D1239454

LANGUAGE CONTACT IN THE AMERICAN DEAF COMMUNITY

LANGUAGE CONTACT
IN THE AMERICAN
DEAF COMMUNITY

Ceil Lucas

Clayton Valli

Department of Linguistics and Interpreting
Gallaudet University
Washington, D.C.

Academic Press, Inc.
Harcourt Brace Jovanovich, Publishers
San Diego   New York   Boston   London   Sydney   Tokyo   Toronto

This book is printed on acid-free paper. ∞

Academic Press, Inc.
1250 Sixth Avenue, San Diego, California 92101-4311

United Kingdom Edition published by
Academic Press Limited
24–28 Oval Road, London NW1 7DX

Library of Congress Cataloging-in-Publication Data

Lucas, Ceil.
    Language contact in the American deaf community / Ceil Lucas and
Clayton Valli.
        p.   cm.
    Includes bibliographical references and index.
    ISBN 0-12-458040-8
    1. Deaf--United States--Means of communication.   2. Sign language.
    3. Pidgin languages--United States.   4. American Sign Language.
    I. Valli, Clayton.   II. Title.
    HV2474.L83   1992
    305.9'08161--dc20   92-4929
                                                                CIP

PRINTED IN THE UNITED STATES OF AMERICA
92 93 94 95 96 97   QW   9 8 7 6 5 4 3 2 1

for Kathleen and Alice
and for the Deaf community:
our professional colleagues, friends, and family.

The best part of human language, properly so called, is derived from reflection on the acts of the mind itself.

Samuel Taylor Coleridge
Biographia Literaria

Contents

CHAPTER   4

Postscript: Implications for Second Language
Learning and Teaching, Interpreting,
and Deaf Education   117

Transcription Conventions

The transcriptions in this volume have three main parts. Signs are represented by English glosses in upper case. On the line above the glosses, nonmanual signals (facial expressions) and eye-gaze are indicated, along with English mouthing that does not match the signs being produced. On a line above the nonmanual signals, the occurrence of mouthing without voice is indicated. Specific symbols used in transcription are as follows:

neg-	head shake
nod-	head nod
nodding-	head nodding
+m -	English mouthing without voice
F̲ROM M̲Y -	first sound of English word corresponding to the sign is produced
"so"-	English mouthing without sign, may be with or without voice
"WELL"-	ASL discourse marker
#, as in #IS-	lexicalized fingerspelling
I-N-K-L-I-N-G	full fingerspelling
[R]ELATIVES	initialized sign (i.e., handshape represents the first letter of the English word)
N	one letter fingerspelled, while English word is mouthed e.g., "non", while signing N

PRO:1	first person
PRO:2	second person
PRO:3	third person, singular
PRO:3pl	third person, plural
NOT	emphasis
gaze	eye gaze
brow	eye brow
/ /	take role
t	topicalization
q	yes/no question
rhet-q	rhetorical question
INDEX-rt ⎱ INDEX-lf ⎰	signed simultaneously on right and left
IMP-	incomplete sign e.g., IMPACT not fully signed
DET	determiner

Preface

In the fall of 1990, the deaf students in an undergraduate-level linguistics course on the structure of American Sign Language (ASL) were asked in their dialogue journals with the teacher which languages they use and if they know and use more than one language. Most of the students responded that they use ASL, English for reading and writing, and also what has been labeled PSE (Pidgin Sign English). They were then asked to explain the difference between ASL and PSE, or contact signing, as we will refer to it in this book. One student wrote:

> Contact signing is mixed ASL and English at the same time. Contact signing includes English words in spelling, partially ASL, not exactly English but English and ASL at the same time. ASL is a language and has structure, while contact sign has a mixed structure and system. It is a mixed language.

Another student wrote:

> PSE is partly SEE language* and partly ASL. I can see that PSE is not fully signed in ASL because of a lot of lip movement and some verbs like "ing," "ed," etc.

*Signing Exact English, one of the codes devised for representing English manually. These codes are often referred to as Manually Coded English or MCE.

Finally, another student simply wrote:

> PSE . . . is a mixture of MCE and ASL.

These undergraduates clearly have fairly sophisticated metalinguistic intuitions about one of the outcomes of language contact in the American deaf community,[†] namely a kind of signing that results from the contact between ASL and English and exhibits features of both languages.

The project on which this book is based began in the summer of 1986 as a linguistic and sociolinguistic investigation of this contact signing. The project's original goals were actually quite straightforward: to look at contact signing and to reexamine claims that it is a pidgin and the result of deaf–hearing interaction. Our objectives were to implement a data-collection methodology to elicit the production of this kind of signing, and to describe the linguistic and sociolinguistic features of this signing. The original goal was to focus specifically on earlier claims that had been made, hence the preoccupation with the term *pidgin* and its relevance to the outcome of language contact in the American deaf community. That is, the project started out as an investigation of and a response to very specific earlier claims about the outcome of one kind of language contact in the American deaf community. And this book does indeed attempt to answer those claims and stands as a concluding description of the project and of our findings.

However, as work on the project and on this book progressed, our research questions multiplied and became less straightforward than we had anticipated, and our list of goals necessarily grew longer. We were forced to step back and take a look at the much larger picture of language contact in the American deaf community in general and to consider issues somewhat broader than those addressed by the project. That is, the conclusions that we have reached about language contact in the American deaf community are based necessarily upon the data that we collected, but those data reflect only several of the many possible contact situations that

---

[†]Upper-case *Deaf* is used by researchers to refer to individuals who are culturally deaf, while lower-case *deaf* is used to refer to audiological deafness. We use both forms in this volume because not all participants in language contact situations are culturally deaf.

occur in the deaf community. Later entries in the student dialogue journals illustrate the situation we were faced with. For example, one student wrote:

> I use . . . ASL, Signed English, and very little PSE. The reason for this is that my signs vary from group to group and I adjust myself accordingly to the person or persons I am associated with.

When asked if contact signing was ever used between deaf people when no hearing people are around, one student replied:

> Sure! Deaf people do use contact sign with each other—perhaps they were having an intellectual discussion using all those vocabulary terms! Sometimes deaf people do feel more comfortable using contact sign.

Clearly, the students had intuitions not only about the linguistic features of the language they use but also about the effect of the situation and participants on their linguistic choices.

As our project progressed, it became necessary to address broader issues concerning language contact in the American deaf community, issues that went beyond the original research questions. We found ourselves going beyond the initial focus of the project—that is, whether this kind of signing is rightly labeled a *pidgin*—to other issues. Such issues include not only the linguistic features of contact signing but the situation in which it is used and the fact that its use is not restricted to deaf–hearing interaction, the nature of the outcome of language contact in situations different from the ones we examined, the parallels between language contact outcomes in spoken language situations and sign language situations, the history of language contact in the American deaf community, and the implications of our study both for a larger theory of language contact and for areas of practical application such as education, second-language teaching, and interpreting.

In short, we found that the story we had to tell was much longer and somewhat different than we had thought it would be. This book, then, is an attempt to address these issues and to situate the specific findings of our investigation within the much larger context of language contact in general and language contact in the American deaf communities in particular. We describe the outcome of one kind of language contact situation in this community. There are many language contact situations in the American deaf community and in deaf communities around the world, the outcomes of which we have only speculated upon, since no empirical data exist yet for many of these situations. It is our hope that our speculation will inspire others to collect data in these situations and to describe their sociolinguistic features and linguistic outcomes.

Finally, we feel that it is important to point out that we have been writing about and presenting our findings since 1986. As we have collected more data and continued our analysis, our focus on our findings has necessarily become sharper and our perspective on some of our earlier findings has necessarily broadened and changed. This book simply reflects our current understanding of our data. We have no doubt that the understanding will grow and change with time.

In Chapter 1, we review research that has been done on contact both in spoken language and sign language situations, describe the characteristics of the deaf community relevant to an understanding of language contact, and present a model of the linguistic outcomes of language contact in the deaf community. In Chapter 2, we describe our study of contact signing: how we collected the data, what patterns of language use emerged from the data, the issue of judgments, and the linguistic features of contact signing based on our data. Chapter 3 considers our findings in terms of language contact in general, and Chapter 4 discusses some of the implications of our findings for deaf education, second-language teaching, and interpreting.

Acknowledgments

Many people contributed to making the publication of this volume possible and we would like to recognize them. First of all, the project would not have been possible without the support of Michael A. Karchmer, Dean of Graduate Studies and Research, and Njeri Nuru, Dean of the School of Communication, both at Gallaudet University. We are also grateful to our colleagues in the Department of Linguistics and Interpreting at Gallaudet University, in particular Robert E. Johnson and Scott K. Liddell, who read and gave detailed feedback on parts of the manuscript, and Carol Patrie, who gave us the opportunity to present our preliminary findings on several occasions. We thank members of the Gallaudet Department of TV, Film and Photography, in particular Eleanor Galloway, Dave Hall, and Nathan Blanton, for allowing us to use the television studios for interviews, and especially Laura Harvey whose technical wizardry produced our judgment tape. We also thank Norman Ingram, Ruth Reed, Diane Ollie-Coleman, Eloise Molock, Su Crutchfield, Kevin Clarke, and Donna Pope for assisting in the data collection and preliminary judgments; Margaret Bibum and Deaf-Pride Inc. for assisting us with the judgment task; Daniel "Chip" Denman of the University of Maryland Statistics Lab for the sample size calculations; Paul Setzer of the Gallaudet University Art Department for the drawings; Harlan Lane, François Grosjean, and Gil

Eastman for comments on the text and information about the early years of deaf education; Nikki Fine and Gayle Early of Academic Press; and Virginia Wulf, Rachel Turniansky, Priscilla "PK" Krisman, and Cheryl Reinagel for manuscript typing.

We are indebted to the 26 individuals who served as our informants and to the researchers, teachers, and members of the Deaf community who served as judges.

We owe a special debt of gratitude to Suzanne Romaine of Oxford University, who thoroughly read and commented on the entire manuscript and provided us with very valuable feedback and perspective.

C H A P T E R   1

What Happens When
Languages Come in Contact

Spoken Language Situations

The Five Foci

The best place for us to begin is by reviewing research on language contact in spoken language situations. This will provide us a framework within which we can examine language contact in sign language situations and will provide an overview of the key issues. Grosjean (1982, p. vii) states that "Bilingualism is present in practically every country of the world, in all classes of society, in all age groups; in fact, it has been estimated that half of the world's population is bilingual." And Mackey (1967, p. 11) observes that "bilingualism, far from being exceptional, is a problem which affects the majority of the world's population." A bilingual situation is by definition a situation in which languages are in contact in some way, and there exists a wide variety of outcomes in language contact situations involving spoken languages.

At least five major foci emerge from an examination of the literature on language contact situations. One focus in language contact studies is on the structural, linguistic outcomes of language contact, including lexical borrowing of various kinds, code switching, code mixing, convergence and divergence, interference, and foreigner talk. A number of studies have looked at these formal consequences of language contact, beginning with Weinreich's 1953 study entitled *Languages in Contact* (Weinreich, 1968) and Haugen's study of Norwegian in the United States published in the same year, and including a vast amount of research, for example, Clyne's work on language contact in Australia (1967, 1972, 1982, 1987); Gumperz and Wilson's work on the effects of Marathi–Urdu–Kannada language contact in Kupwar, India (1971); Poplack's pioneering work on Spanish–English code switching (1980) and subsequent collaboration on descriptions of other language contact situations, including Finnish–English bilinguals, and French–English bilinguals in Canada (Poplack, Wheeler, and Westwood, 1987; Poplack and Sankoff, 1988; Scollon and Scollon's work on Chipewyan and English (1979); Gal's description of German and Hungarian in Austria (1979); Thomason's work in African and Amerindian contact situations (1983, 1984, 1986); Bokamba's studies on Lingala–French contact (1985); Beniak, Mougeon, and Valois' work on Ontarian French (1984/5); Dorian's investigation of Scottish Gaelic (1981); and Scotton's work in Western Kenya (1986). This is by no means a complete inventory of the studies that have been done on linguistic outcomes of language contact in spoken language situations, but it does provide an idea of the range of situations and languages that has been examined. And it should be noted that there is vigorous debate as well concerning the definition of the terms used to characterize the different linguistic outcomes of contact, debate which will be of relevance in our discussion of the deaf community.

A second focus which relates to linguistic outcomes concerns the genetic relations between the languages in a contact situation (Thomason and Kaufman, 1988). That is, are languages which are typologically related likely to have contact outcomes that typologically dissimilar languages will not? Will the contact phenomena that obtain in a French–English situation or a Spanish–English situation differ from those in a Finnish–English situation or a Marathi–Urdu–Kannada situation?

A third focus is on the functions of the respective languages in contact situations, and the various sociolinguistic factors contributing to language maintenance, shift, or death. The foundation for research on this issue was provided by Ferguson's 1959 study of diglossia and was expanded upon by Gumperz (1961, 1962, 1964, 1966) and Fishman (1967, 1972). Some of the studies that focus on the sociolinguistic functions of the languages in contact situations include Rubin's work in Paraguay (1968), Abdulaziz-Mkilifi's examination of diglossia in Tanzania (1978), Platt's work in Malaysia (1977), and Fasold's comprehensive review and discussion of the pertinent theoretical issues (1984). Related to the issue of functions is the issue of the factors involved in the maintenance, shift, and death of languages in contact situations. Romaine (1989, pp. 39–40) provides an extensive examination of these factors which include "numerical strength of the group in relation to other minorities and majorities, social class, religious and educational background, settlement patterns, ties with the homeland, degree of similarity between the majority and minority language, extent of exogamous marriage, attitudes of majority and minority, government policy towards language and education of minorities, and patterns of language use." We will return to a consideration of these factors as they pertain to language contact in the American deaf community.

These factors relate to the fourth focus in language contact studies, that is, the characteristics and the attitudes of the participants in language contact situations—how many and which individuals in a language contact situation are bilingual, how do they become bilingual, what are their attitudes about language contact and bilingualism, and so forth. Key studies which have addressed these questions include Beniak, Mougeon, and Valois' work (1984/5) and Mougeon and Beniak's work (1987) on Ontarian French and Poplack, Sankoff, and Miller's work in the same area (1988).

And related to the fourth focus is a fifth on definitions and measurement of bilingualism and the identification of the languages in a language contact situation. Pioneering studies in this area include Ferguson (1966), Mackey (1968), Lieberson (1969), and Fishman (1972). The literature in this area clearly reveals a lack of consensus among researchers on how bilingualism should be defined or measured. Furthermore, there is often disagreement between researchers and laymen or among laymen as to the actual linguistic status of a particular language—that is, is a given variety most appropriately called a language or a dialect—disagreement which obviously complicates any subsequent description of language contact phenomena.

Themes of Reexamination

These are, then, what appear to be the major foci in studies of contact situations involving spoken languages. In addition to these foci, several related themes consistently emerge from the current language contact literature. Several of these themes are elaborated by Romaine in her volume on bilingualism and are unified by a spirit of reexamination of what we might refer to as the "received knowledge" in bilingualism and language contact studies. By received knowledge we mean that there are a variety of intuitively very attractive ideas that have been "tried on for size" in the course of studying language contact. For example, it perhaps should be that typologically similar languages behave differently in contact situations than typologically different ones; it "sounds right" that a list of constraints on code switching should be able to be identified; it would seem possible to separate the behavior of the individual from the behavior of the group, and so forth. However, what emerge from an examination of the literature are what we might call "themes of reexamination." One such theme is that, given the quality and quantity of factors that come into play in a contact situation, there exist, as Romaine (1989, p. 145) states, "no unambiguous criteria which will decide in all cases what type of language contact phenomenon we are dealing with." Related to this is the ongoing debate over terms used for describing the linguistic outcomes of language contact. That is, is a given phenomenon an example of borrowing or is it more aptly described as code switching; is a given utterance a case of interference or borrowing; what is the precise difference between code switching and code mixing, and so forth.

A second theme is that, given the uniqueness of every situation, the focus in bilingualism and language contact is of necessity not on language but on the user of language, "the recognition of a linguistic system as an autonomous language [being] ultimately a socio-political matter" (Romaine, 1989, p. 283). A related theme is that it would not always seem possible or even desirable to effect a clean separation between individual bilingualism and societal bilingualism, a case in point being the concept of "interference." Grosjean (1989) makes a useful distinction between "static interference" and "dynamic interference." An example of the former would be a "foreign accent," phonological interference from another language which may always be produced by the bilingual, perhaps as a function of the age at which the second language was learned, and which probably cannot be eradicated. Dynamic interference, on the other hand, is episodic and may be caused by such factors as the cognitive and linguistic load, or stress. Romaine (1989, p. 50) states, "What has been called 'interference' is ultimately a product of the bilingual individual's use of more than one language in everyday interaction. At the level of the individual, interference may be sporadic and idiosyncratic. However, over time the effects of interference in a bilingual speech community can be cumulative, and lead to new norms, which are different from those observed by monolinguals who use the language elsewhere." In this regard, Romaine makes the interesting observation that research on bilingualism has, for the most part, been conducted within a framework that views language as "a structured self-contained whole, an autonomous entity which is consistent with itself" (p. 286) and speculates about the nature of linguistic inquiry and theory had it been undertaken by bilinguals in multilingual societies. In the same vein, Grosjean (1992) remarks that " . . . language sciences have developed primarily through the study of monolinguals who have been models of the 'normal' speaker–hearer. The methods of investigation developed to study monolingual speech and language have been used with little, if any, modification to study bilinguals; strong monolingual biases have influenced bilingual research, and the yardstick against which bilinguals have been measured has inevitably been the ideal-monolingual-speaker–hearer." A final reexamination theme concerns the recognition of bilingual and contact situations as dynamic as opposed to static events. This theme relates to the aforementioned recognition of the user being, as Romaine (1989) observes, the locus of contact and, more precisely, the user's interaction with other users.

We will see that the study of bilingualism and language contact in the American deaf community has itself been the recipient of some received knowledge and that many of the earlier characterizations of the situation merit reexamination. Indeed, it was in the

spirit of reexamining claims about the outcome of language contact
as a pidgin that this volume got its start. We will see that each of the
themes of reexamination that we have described has direct bearing
on our description of language contact in the American deaf community. To arrive at a description of the outcomes of language
contact, however, we must first look at the characteristics of the
community itself.

The American Deaf Community

The Participants and the Codes in Question

To understand the outcome of language contact in the American
deaf community, a great number of factors must be taken into
consideration. While it is true that the two languages in question are
ASL and English, the outcome of contact between the two languages is shaped by the characteristics of the users in a contact
situation and by the varieties of language available to those users.
There are many different kinds of bilinguals in the American deaf
community. For example, there are audiologically deaf adults
whose parents are hearing and did not sign to their children. Typically, these deaf adults attended residential schools for the deaf
(entering the school, say, at age three or four), learned ASL from
their peers, and were taught some form of English, usually by hearing teachers who did not sign natively. And typically, the use of
ASL was forbidden in the classrooms of these schools, while being
permitted or tolerated in the dorms. Other deaf adults have Deaf
families and acquired ASL natively from their parents. Many of
these individuals also attended residential schools and had the role
of language models for their peers from hearing families. These
individuals have usually been exposed to English by their parents
at home, along with ASL, but at this point, the evidence of signed
or spoken English in the home is largely anecdotal. For example, a
Gallaudet undergraduate whose parents are Deaf and who signs
ASL as a first language observed in a dialogue journal, "At first
when I was born, my parents thought I was hearing due to *very* little
hearing loss. Afraid that I may have poor speech and English skills,

they decided to use straight English and their voices whenever talking to me." Later her parents went back to using ASL. And another student, the daughter of Deaf parents and the fifth generation of Deaf people in her family, explains that when SEE was introduced in the 1970s, her mother learned the system and placed her in a mainstream program. Another Deaf student from a Deaf family tells of how her parents put English labels on all of the household items—CHAIR, LAMP, and so forth—so that she would learn to read English as early as possible. To date, however, sociolinguistic and ethnographic data to support the anecdotal observations do not exist. Still other deaf adults may have hearing parents and may have been sent to mainstream programs. As a result, they may have learned to sign relatively late—ASL or signed English— and they may have been exposed to whatever form of signing they learned by interpreters or teachers, themselves perhaps non-native signers.

It is important to notice that thus far in our account of the participants in language contact situations, we have focused on deaf *adults* and the sociolinguistic background that they bring with them to contact situations. Their linguistic behavior in contact situations is directly related to the traditional roles assigned to ASL and English in deaf education. Most well known, of course, are the developments following the Congress of Milan in 1880, at which the use of sign language in deaf education was condemned in favor of oralist methods. The result for American education was that ASL was considered inappropriate as a medium of instruction and expressly forbidden in many settings. The early 1970s witnessed the development of signed English systems but not the use of ASL. However, the relationship between English and ASL in the deaf community certainly did not begin with the advent of oralism in the 1880s. In the first place, it would indeed be a challenge to find a sign language anywhere in the world that did not have some kind of contact with the spoken language of the community surrounding it, whatever the outcomes of that contact might be. That is, the contact might not necessarily have structural consequences for the sign language in question. But a deaf community exhibiting no contact with the majority spoken language community, if it exists, would be marked by a remarkable degree of isolation. And we can safely assume that American deaf people who lived in the United States and used ASL prior to the formal beginning of deaf education in 1817 had some contact with English.

One example of this is provided by Groce in her account of the situation on Martha's Vineyard (1985). As is well known, Martha's Vineyard Island had a high incidence of hereditary deafness for over 200 years—the last hereditary deaf person died in 1952—and what is unique about the situation is that almost all of the residents, hearing and deaf alike, used sign language. Groce points out that for the first several decades after the American Asylum was founded in Hartford, "the single largest group of deaf children seems to have been from Martha's Vineyard. No other area sent anywhere near so many children to Hartford, and most of the other students had grown up in small towns and rural areas, knowing few or no other deaf children." (Groce, 1985, p. 73; she also cites American Annals of the Deaf, 1852; and Clerc, 1818). Her focus, of course, is on the relationship between the sign language being used in Hartford and the sign language used in Martha's Vineyard, the latter possibly having its origins in the British sign language used in Kent.

As concerns the relationship between ASL and English, it is simply interesting to notice that the Martha's Vineyard children themselves came from a completely bilingual community in which hearing and deaf alike used sign language and no doubt brought any contact outcomes of this situation with them to Hartford. Furthermore, we know a fair amount about the actual methods of teaching English in the earliest days of deaf education and we know that there was explicit and overt representation of English structure with signs. As is well known, the method for teaching deaf students which had been devised in France by L'Epée and which formed the basis of the method first implemented in the United States by Gallaudet and Laurent Clerc included the use of so-called "methodical signs" in conjunction with natural signs. These methodical signs were signs invented to represent the parts of French inflectional and derivational morphology such as tense, gender, derivational affixes, prepositions, and articles that have no counterparts in French Sign Language structure, as well as French words for which no signs existed. An example is as follows: "To express something past, our pupil used to move his hand negligently toward his shoulder. We tell him he must move it just once for the imperfect, twice for the perfect, and three times for the past perfect . . . . We raise our hand to our hat for the masculine and to our ear, where a woman's bonnet ends, for the feminine" (Lane, 1984, p. 61). Lane (1984, p. 62) explains the basic steps in Epée's method as follows:

> The pupil would first learn the manual alphabet, one handshape for each letter in French, so he could fingerspell French words. Next he would learn to write these letters and then to write out the conjugation of a verb . . . . To provide him with a few nouns, Epée began with some twenty parts of the body that could be singled out by pointing, and he associated with each the French name of that part written on a card. The pupil would learn to spell those names with letter cutouts. Next he was taught the methodical signs for the persons and tenses of the verb he had conjugated, as well as a few signs for articles and prepositions. Now he could write his first sentence in French in response to dictation in methodical signs. From here on in, the list of nouns and verbs and methodical signs grew.

Lane states that Laurent Clerc espoused the same method at the American School for the Deaf (originally known as the Institution for Deaf-Mutes and subsequently as the Connecticut Asylum for the Education and Instruction of Deaf and Dumb Persons, founded in 1817 by Thomas Hopkins Gallaudet and Clerc) but gradually abandoned it. In this regard, Lane (1984, p. 63) quotes Clerc:

> It took the genius of Sicard's disciple and successor, Roch-Ambroise Bébian, to help us realize that all this was a needless encumbrance on our instruction, that the labor involved in teaching the . . . methodical signs was the very labor required to teach the corresponding English sentence. There was no need for the intermediate step of manual English. And so increasingly we presented the idea in American Sign Language and then turned at once to the written language. By the 1830s methodical signs had disappeared on both sides of the Atlantic.

He goes on to explain that three forms of communication were eventually used in the classroom—American Sign Language, written English, and fingerspelling, the latter being the French Manual Alphabet brought to America by Clerc. As far as language contact is concerned, it is important to have a clear picture of what the actual communication situation was at the American School for the Deaf at its inception, since it was by no means monolithic and since the school played such a key role in shaping communication in the Deaf community. Consider, for example, the language backgrounds of some of the teachers and students of the very first class: Alice

Cogswell, age 11 at the time of the founding, whose language use Lane describes as "a mixture of her own home sign, pantomime, and fingerspelling with the two-handed British manual alphabet" (1984, p. 179); Parnel and Sophie Fowler, two deaf sisters who apparently had a system of home signs; John Brewster, a painter who entered the school at age 51 and of whom it was remarked that he could "write well and converse in signs" (a remark, as Gannon points out, made in 1790, 26 years before the arrival of Clerc, suggesting the existence of at least some small deaf communities in the United States at that time) (Gannon, 1981, p. 359); three young boys—George Loring, Wilson Whiton, and Levi Backus, with apparently no prior contact with signing or deaf people; and of course Laurent Clerc and Thomas Hopkins Gallaudet. Clerc knew French Sign Language and the methodical signs for French, as well as English; Gallaudet was a native English speaker and had learned some French Sign Language as well as methodical signs for written French. And Clerc reports that he and Gallaudet adapted many of the French methodical signs for the instruction of English (Lane, 1984, p. 226). Our point is simply that the communication system at the very beginning of the school was fairly complex. It was not as though there was only one language being used by students and teachers. It is clear that, at the beginning, teachers and students brought with them a variety of linguistic backgrounds, all of which came together to form a system shared by the school community.

Although in the early years natural sign language was the medium of instruction and some of the teachers were themselves both audiologically and culturally deaf (Gannon, 1981), the situation began to change even prior to the Congress of Milan, as the central roles of English and speech were visibly championed and restored in deaf education. The point, however, is that ASL and English were in close contact long before 1880, and that contact was both the natural contact of two languages existing in the same geographical space and the more contrived contact resulting from the quite self-conscious adaptation of a spoken language to visual means. In addition, the contact situation is made even more complex by the fact that even though the methodical signs were abandoned, there remained some signs which had started out as initialized signs in French Sign Language—that is, resulting from the contact between natural French sign language and written French, contact which produced outcomes long before Gallaudet arrived in France—and which made their way into ASL. Examples include the signs SEARCH, GOOD, and DOCTOR, all ASL signs which have handshapes that reflect the first letter of the *French* written word—C (*chercher*), B (*bon*), and M (*medecin*), respectively. Furthermore, there is some evidence that some of the methodical signs invented to represent parts of English structure made their way into ASL even though the system of methodical signs was abandoned. For example, Lane (1984, pp. 213, 226) presents evidence that signs were invented for French and English prepositions, words the grammatical function of which is usually fulfilled in ASL by classifier predicates. Now, in modern ASL, there exist signs IN, ON, UNDER, BEHIND, and TO, that is, the phonological forms exist. However, these signs are not usually used in the same way prepositions are used in English or French. The grammatical relationships shown in English with the words *in, on, under, behind,* and *to* are accomplished in ASL with classifier predicates and use of the signing space. So the phonological forms exist but they do not usually occur in prepositional phrases as they do in English. They may have other functions in ASL. For example, the sign BEHIND occurs in the compound MONEY BEHIND, meaning *savings,* and the sign IN can be produced on the chest with the meaning of "integral part of my being." Not that spoken language prepositions never acquire other syntactic functions; they do, as in the expressions "to up the ante" or "to down a cup of coffee." What's interesting in the ASL case is that it appears that signs were invented expressly for English prepositions with prepositional function and are either not used as such or have acquired other functions.

Finally, there is another interesting fact about deaf education in the nineteenth century that may have some relevance for understanding the early ASL–English contact situation. Lou (1988) points out that the minimum age for admission to the Hartford school in 1817 was 14 years, which later dropped to 12 and then to 8 by 1843. Brill (1974) reports that the average age of the last 100 students entering the school in 1893 was 10.8 years. As Lou (1988) states, "throughout this period the students were predominantly adolescents, not young children" (p. 81). Furthermore, she points out that the percentage of *congenitally* deaf children increased and decreased over the years. The percentage of congenitally deaf children at Hartford in 1844 was 44%, as compared to 57.4% in 1880 (based on census reports), 41.5% in 1910 (based on census reports), and 69% in 1970, as reported by Ries (1973). As Lou reports, the change in the number of congenitally deaf children had an impact on the structure of educational programs: "The decrease in the proportion of congenital deafness through the early decades of this century . . . appears to have occurred at the same time that pure oral approaches dominated. The recent increase in the proportion of congenital deafness occurs at a time when manual approaches are back in vogue" (pp. 89–90).

What is of interest for the ASL-English contact situation is that, based on these statistics, many of the students in the early years at Hartford may have in fact been adventitiously deaf, and hence native English speakers. Table 1 (adapted from Moores, 1987, who in turn adapted it from Weld, 1844) shows the causes of deafness in students at the American School for the Deaf, 1817–1844. Moores states that "it may be assumed the majority of students in the 'acquired' category had achieved some level of proficiency in speech and English before losing their hearing, leading to the conclusion that the composition of the 'deaf population' of the American School from 1817 to 1844 was different from that of schools for the deaf today, a large majority of whose students either were born deaf or lost their hearing before the acquisition of language" (Moores, 1987, p. 85). Lou reports that many young deaf children were not sent to school in the early years because public state schools were residential and unable to accept very young children, so that may account for part of the situation at Hartford. That is, there may have been students there who were indeed born deaf but simply did not enroll until a later age. But the possible presence of many students who were already English speakers at the time that they became deaf casts an interesting light on the teaching of English, the teaching and learning of ASL, and the interaction of ASL and English.

For one, English was probably being taught to some students who could already speak it. Second, this was at least in part an environment that included native English speakers learning ASL. In addition to adventitiously deaf students, many of the teachers in the early years were hearing. While there were indeed many deaf teachers between 1817 and 1860, Lou (1988) states that "Between 1817 and the 1860s teachers in schools for the Deaf were typically

TABLE 1
Causes of Deafness in Students at the
American School for the Deaf, 1817–1844[a]

Category	Former students	In attendance in 1844	Total
Acquired			
Fever			
Spotted fever	45	1	46
Scarlet fever	20	22	44 (sic)
Fever	29	6	35
Typhus fever	11	1	12
Lung fever	1	1	2
Yellow fever	1	0	1
Sickness	76	8	84
Inflammation in head	24	6	30
Ulcers in head	14	8	22
Accidents	10	12	22
Measles	11	1	12
Whooping cough	8	4	12
Dropsy	5	0	5
Fits	2	2	4
Smallpox	2	0	2
Palsy	2	0	2
Croup	1	0	1
Total Acquired	262	72	336
Congenital	270	71	341
Unknown	87	9	96
Total	619	152	773

[a]Adapted from Moores (1987).

male college graduates who learned to teach their deaf pupils through on-the-job training, with additional special instruction in Sign Language. The faculty at the American Asylum learned Sign Language from Laurent Clerc, and from their ranks came most of the principals and teachers of the other schools for the Deaf" (p. 81). As Harlan Lane points out (personal communication, 1991), the students at Hartford also interacted with members of the larger hearing community in the city of Hartford as well. Given all of these factors, it seems reasonable to say that there was extensive natural ASL–English contact, not limited to classroom settings involving the instruction of English, and there may have existed a form of contact signing from the earliest days. In addition, many Hartford graduates themselves went on to found schools for the deaf or teach at schools for the deaf (Gannon, 1981). This means that the outcomes of language contact at Hartford may have been transported to other places, in addition to the ASL–English contact taking place on its own in those locales.

The issue here is that language contact in the American deaf community has a long and unique history. It is unique because it is not simply the history of contact between the users of two languages or the tidy story of the respective functions of two languages in a given situation. The conclusion from a superficial examination might simply conclude that there were ASL users and English users, and ASL and English were in contact because of their respective roles in education and in the community. One might imagine that there were deaf children who had never heard English who were being taught English by deaf and hearing teachers and that the linguistic outcomes were the result of that contact situation. And certainly that kind of contact situation exists in the deaf community. But the uniqueness of the Hartford situation lies precisely with the users, many of whom, it would appear, started out as native English speakers, became deaf as children or adolescents, and learned ASL. This is a very different kind of contact situation and understanding the details of it helps us to understand the linguistic and sociolinguistic outcomes of language contact today. The details of the historical situation also challenge the commonly accepted view that contact signing is strictly the result of deaf–hearing interaction, to accommodate the fact that hearing people don't understand ASL. It might be that the earliest manifestation of contact signing was produced by hearing people who had become deaf. That is, the contact signing didn't incorporate features of English necessarily because the hearing people couldn't understand ASL. It might have incorporated features of English because the first language of some of its users *was* English, even though they were now learning ASL.

It would appear that language contact in the American deaf community has had some clear linguistic and sociolinguistic conse-

quences for ASL that persist despite changes in educational phil-
osophy and methodology. It has also resulted in a unique form of
signing which we refer to as contact signing, the description of
which was the goal of our project. At present, the respective roles
of English and ASL (or of a spoken language and a natural sign
language) are again being seriously questioned by many educators,
parents of deaf children, and members of the deaf community, and
programs in which children learn curriculum content through a
natural sign language and the spoken language of the community as
a second language are being implemented all over the world. The
result of these changes in the role of natural sign languages in deaf
education will have an inevitable effect on what happens in language contact situations, so that an adult's behavior in a contact
situation may differ from that of a child. The linguistic behavior in
contact situations of a generation of children instructed in ASL with
English as a second language, with expanded functions for ASL,
and with a clear and early metalinguistic awareness of ASL cannot
help but differ from the behavior of individuals educated in the
traditional way, for example, with no metalinguistic awareness of
ASL and a frequent perception that any kind of English-based signing is preferable in many settings to ASL and contributes to the
perception of the signer as educated and intelligent.

Other participants in a language contact situation may be the
hearing children of deaf parents, once again ASL–English bilinguals who acquired ASL at home natively. They may be hearing
native English speakers who learned ASL or some variety of Signed
English relatively late in life. The ability of members of this group
to hear is an important variable in language contact situations. As
we will see, deaf individuals not only can sign quite differently with
other deaf individuals than with hearing individuals but can also
initiate an interaction in one language and radically shift when the
interlocutor's ability to hear is revealed. For example, a Deaf native
ASL user may initiate an interaction with another individual whom
he believes to be deaf or whose audiological status has not been
clarified. The latter participant may well be a near-native user of
ASL. Once the latter's hearing ability becomes apparent, however,
it is not unusual for the deaf participant to automatically stop using
ASL and begin using an English-based form of signing. Other participants in language contact situations may be late-deafened adults

who are native English users learning to sign, hearing individuals who are English monolinguals and do not sign, deaf ASL monolinguals with a minimal command of English in any form. Similarly, the varieties of language available to participants in a contact situation include ASL, spoken English, signed English, and a variety of codes devised for representing English manually and implemented in educational settings. These codes are commonly referred to as Manually Coded English or MCE.

The motivation for the invention of these codes has traditionally been that deaf children should be provided with a visual model of English, and their use has been widespread in American deaf education since the early 1970s. Johnson, Liddell, and Erting (1989) introduced the term "sign-supported speech" (SSS) to refer to the simultaneous use of spoken English and signs, as occurs with Signed English or MCEs. They state that "speech is seen as the primary signal in the conglomerate of signing and speaking. A large proportion of the signs used in SSS are special signs developed for use with spoken English" (1989, p. 5). Of crucial importance to an understanding of the contact situation is the fact that while the various manifestations of SSS include signs, they are entirely distinct from ASL, a natural language with an autonomous grammar that is completely independent from the grammar of English and from the systems devised to represent English manually. Finally, it is important to realize that the participants in a language contact situation have both the vocal channel and the visual channel available, the latter including both manual and nonmanual grammatical signals. That is, the participants in a language contact situation have hands, mouth, body, and face available for the encoding of linguistic messages.

In Lucas and Valli (1989, p. 13), we proposed a partial list of the possible language contact situations that might occur in the American deaf community, according to participant characteristics. We reproduce it here:

- Deaf bilinguals with hearing bilinguals
- Deaf bilinguals with Deaf bilinguals
- Deaf bilinguals with hearing spoken English monolinguals
- Hearing bilinguals with deaf English signers
- Deaf bilinguals with deaf English signers

- deaf English signers with hearing spoken English monolinguals
- deaf English signers with hearing bilinguals
- deaf English signers with deaf ASL monolinguals
- Deaf bilinguals with deaf ASL monolinguals
- Deaf ASL monolinguals with hearing bilinguals

One issue that emerges from this list, of course, is what we mean by *bilingual*. It is clear that the two languages in question are ASL and English, but the term *bilingual* would appear to be relative within the context of the deaf community. Grosjean (1992) discusses the difficulty in seeing a bilingual simply as the sum of two complete or incomplete monolinguals, and that observation certainly has relevance for the deaf community. For example, the label *hearing bilinguals* would generally include hearing people who have a command of ASL (either because they have deaf parents and acquired it natively or because they learned it as a second language in adulthood) and of spoken and written English. However, many deaf adults with a firm command of written English choose not to use their voices because they are not able to hear themselves and hence monitor the volume or pitch of their speech. As we will see in the description of our videotaped data, many deaf adults will mouth English words or sentences in contact situations, but this mouthing will occur without voice. This situation would seem to necessitate reconsideration of the term *bilingual*: It is clear that in the American deaf community, command of two languages does not necessarily include *speaking* the languages in question, at least not in the way that the term *speaking* is generally understood by linguists. In fact, Grosjean (1992) points out the parallel between bilinguals in a spoken language minority/majority situation and bilinguals in a sign language situation and observes that minority language speakers in both situations may exhibit varying levels of competence in the majority language. The interesting difference that we find is that while people in spoken language situations may have varying competence in the majority language due to a variety of *sociolinguistic* factors—for example, restricted access to the majority language for social reasons—a key factor in a sign language situation may be simply *physiological*. That is, a deaf adult may not have competence in the spoken language simply because he cannot *hear* it and not because sociolinguistic factors are restricting access (see also Grosjean, 1982, p. 88). Finally, as we mentioned earlier, there exist deaf adults who have learned to sign relatively late in life and do not have a command of ASL, their signing having a more English-like structure. This, then, is the reason for our use of the term *deaf English signers*. We will return to the issue of redefinition of terms later.

The second issue that emerges from this list relates to Grosjean's (1982) observation that what happens when a bilingual interacts with a monolingual may be different from what happens when a bilingual interacts with another bilingual, hence our inclusion of both monolinguals and bilinguals. Our list shows how complex the language contact situation in the American deaf community can be. We turn our attention now to a review of how this language contact situation has been described.

How Language Contact Has Been Described

In the first section of this chapter, we discussed five different areas that have been focused upon in studies of spoken language contact: the linguistic outcomes of language contact, the genetic relations between the languages in question, the respective functions of the languages in question, the characteristics and attitudes of the participants, and definitions and measurement of bilingualism. With one exception, the same areas have been focused upon in descriptions of sign language situations.

Given the variety in both participant characteristics and languages available, it is not surprising that one linguistic outcome of language contact in the deaf community is something that cannot be strictly described as ASL or as a signed representation of English. Several studies have looked specifically at this particular linguistic outcome. Contact signing is characterized as "an interface between deaf signers and hearing speakers" by Fischer (1978, p. 314) and is labeled Pidgin Sign English (PSE) by Woodward (1972, 1973b). The linguistic characteristics of this so-called PSE were examined in three studies: Woodward (1973b), Woodward and Markowicz (1975), and Reilly and McIntire (1980). Woodward (1973b, p. 17) states that "sometimes people sign something that seems to be a pidginized version of English. The syntactic order is primarily

English, but inflections have been reduced in redundancy, and there is a mixture of American Sign Language and English structure." Later in his discussion, he states:

> These characteristics point up some close similarities between PSE and other pidgins. In most pidgins, articles are deleted; the copula is usually uninflected; inflections such as English plural are lost and most derivations are lost, just as they are in PSE. Perfective aspect in pidgins is often expressed through *finish* or a similar verb like *done*. [p. 42]

Woodward (1973b) and Woodward and Markowicz (1975) provide a description of some of the linguistic characteristics of PSE, which appear in Table 2. This inventory includes what they call agent–beneficiary directionality, negative incorporation, and number incorporation, and they also mention aspects of PSE phonology, specifically handshapes, location, and movement.

Reilly and McIntire (1980, p. 151) define PSE as "a form of signing used by many hearing people for interacting with deaf people and thus is a commonly encountered dialect of ASL." They point out (1980, p. 152) that

> . . . although PSE has been classified as a pidgin language, it differs from most pidgins in important ways . . . . Syntactically, PSE does not appear as many other pidgins. Because it does make use of a number of English grammatical devices for creating complex sentences, it has access to a wider range of grammatical constructions than do most pidgins.

Other researchers have described the linguistic outcome of language contact in other terms. For example, Cokely (1983, pp. 11, 20) states that the ASL–English contact situation

> . . . can be described as one in which members of the Deaf community communicate with hearing people in a foreigner talk register of ASL, and members of the hearing community communicate with Deaf people in a foreigner talk register of English . . . . The ASL–English contact situation does not, in fact, result in the emergence of a pidgin. Although the process of pidginization may be detected in the ASL–English situation, the preconditions for the development of a pidgin language are not adequately met. Instead the variation along the ASL–English continuum of varieties or registers can be accounted for by the dynamic interplay of foreigner talk, judgments of proficiency, and learner's attempts to master the target language—whether this is ASL for hearing users or English for Deaf users.

TABLE 2
Linguistic Characteristics of Pidgin Sign English (PSE)[a]

Feature	ASL	Sign English	PSE
Articles	No	Yes	Variable: A, T-H-E (fingerspelled)
Plurality	Noun pluralization by reduplication	-s, etc.	Some reduplication, generally does not use marker to represent English s plural
Copula	No	Yes	With older signers, represented by the sign TRUE.
Progressive	Verb reduplication	-ing	"PSE retains verb reduplication in a few heavily weighted environments, e.g., 'run,' 'drive.' PSE uninflected copula or inflected forms plus a verb for Standard English be + ing. PSE, however, drops the redundant + ing" (Woodward, 1973b; p. 41).
Perfective	FINISH		FINISH$_2$, an allomorph of ASL FINISH

[a]From Lucas & Valli (1989).

A recent description of one aspect of the contact situation (the interaction of native ASL signers with hearing nonnative signers) in terms of foreigner talk was undertaken by Myles-Zitzer (1990), who examined the input of a native ASL signer to two hearing second-language learners of ASL and to one native ASL signer. She adapted the foreigner-talk registral characteristics postulated by Ferguson and DeBose (1977) to sign language, and concluded that

> ... the accommodations made by a native signer to hearing nonnative second language learners of ASL can be characterized by the dynamic interplay of foreigner-talk, judgments of proficiency, and learner's grammar. This characterization is further defined by universal processes of pidginization which arise under conditions of restricted input in relation to perceptual-linguistic constraints of the learner, including a limited knowledge of the target language norm as well as limited socio-cultural experience. [p. 202]

Other researchers have examined other outcomes of language contact in the American deaf community. For example, Meadow (1972), Bernstein, Maxwell, and Matthews (1985), Aramburo (1989), and Hayes (1990) discuss code switching (the latter in a study of the historical roles of English and ASL in the communication, education, and culture of deaf people in America), and Battison (1978) described fingerspelling as a form of lexical borrowing. Battison discusses the ASL–English contact situation in general and distinguishes artificial influences on ASL from natural influences. Artificial influences include

> a number of contrived signing systems which have been developed by their authors to encode English more exactly . . . These systems rely on the contrivance of new signs or the modification of existing signs to correspond to (one or many) uses of an English word, invented signs to correspond to the inflectional and derivational morphology of English, and extensive initialization of many existing ASL signs[1] to make the relationship between a sign and a given English word more salient and more explicit. [Battison, 1978, p. 97]

He notes that some of the contrived and initialized signs have made their way into the adult deaf community through the schools for the deaf where they are introduced: "A number of frequently occurring signs are initialized. In color signs, only BLACK, WHITE, and RED are non-initialized signs; RED has an initialized variant, and BLUE, GREEN, YELLOW, PURPLE, PINK, etc. are always initialized. With the exception of Sunday, all days of the week are initialized" (Battison, 1978, p. 98). Natural influences on ASL include (1) the use of English morphology and syntax, especially regarding sign order: "This strategy is used extensively in deaf–hearing contact situations, limited of course by the signer's or the receiver's knowledge of English syntax and morphology" (Battison, 1978, p. 99); (2) loan translation, in which an existing ASL sign takes on the semantic properties of one of its English glosses; (3) fingerspelled words; and (4) fingerspelled words which develop specialized meanings and systematic mutations of forms, approximating the forms of signs. The latter are the focus of Battison's (1978) study of lexical borrow-

---

1. Initialization of signs is the process whereby the handshape of the sign represents the first letter of the English orthographic system, as in *TEAM*, *READY*, or *FAMILY*, each with a T, R, or F handshape respectively.

ing. He states that "in contact situations involving spoken language, words are borrowed from one language into another and undergo phonological, morphological, and semantic restructurings that make them more compatible with the structural properties of the borrowing language" (p. 105), and claims that the situation is analogous for loan signs originating in fingerspelled words. More recently, Davis (1989) investigated language contact phenomena in ASL interpretation, specifically mouthing, fingerspelling, and flagging. We will return to a discussion of his findings in a later section.[2]

We said that all of the foci identified in spoken language contact studies can be found in sign language studies, with one exception. That one exception is the second focus discussed, genetic relations between languages in a contact situation. Although some researchers have explored the historical relationship between two sign languages—for example, French Sign Language and American Sign Language (Woodward and DeSantis, 1977; DeSantis, 1977)—it can probably be said that, at this point, simply not enough is known about the history and structure of individual natural sign languages, much less about genetic relations between sign languages and the effect of those relations on the outcome of language contact.

Researchers have investigated the third focus, the relative functions of the respective languages in a contact situation. For example, the suggestion that Ferguson's (1959) concept of diglossia might be applicable to the deaf community was first made by Stokoe (1969). By the low (L) variety, Stokoe was referring to ASL. As he (Stokoe, 1969, p. 23) states, "The H (superposed or 'high') variety is English. However, this English is a form most unfamiliar to usual linguistic scrutiny. It is not spoken but uttered in 'words' which are fingerspelled or signed." The characterization of the situation as diglossic meant that ASL was used in some contexts and a more English-like signing was used in other contexts, with no overlap. In reexamining this characterization of the situation, Lee (1982, p. 27) states that although "there is indeed variation [in the deaf community] . . . code-switching and style shifting rather than

---

2. It should be noted that research on the outcomes of language contact in deaf communities is certainly not limited to the United States. For example, Schermer (1990) has examined the influence of spoken Dutch on Netherlands Sign Language, and Deuchar (1985) has examined language contact in British Sign Language (BSL).

diglossia appear to be the norm." Three of Ferguson's (1959) nine criteria for diglossia are linguistic (lexicon, phonology, and grammar), while six are described by Lee as sociolinguistic (literary heritage, standardization, prestige, stability, acquisition, and function). As Lee (1982, p. 147) observes, "I have found none of the nine characteristics actually consistent with diglossia, at least in some parts of the linguistic community." Nevertheless, as she goes on to point out, "The concept of a sign language 'continuum' linking the H and L varieties . . . has become quite popular. This continuum represents a scale of all of the varieties of ASL and English produced by both deaf and hearing signers. These varieties imperceptibly grade into ASL on one extreme and English on the other" (1982, p. 131). This characterization of the outcome of language contact as a diglossic continuum has been widely accepted in the American deaf community by professionals and laymen alike (see also Deuchar, 1985, on diglossia in the BSL community).

In terms of the fourth focus, there are a number of studies that have looked at the characteristics and attitudes of the participants in bilingual situations in the American deaf community. For example, in writing about cultural conflicts between hearing and deaf communities, Padden and Markowicz (1976) observe that deafness itself does not ensure entry into the deaf community, and that appropriate language skills and behaviors are also necessary. Hence, language attitudes are a key component in acceptance or non-acceptance. Bergman (1976) and Meath-Lang (1978) examined deaf students' attitudes toward the teaching and the teachers of English, while Berke (1978) looked at deaf high school students' attitudes toward ASL. Ward-Trotter (1989) adapted the matched guise method used in spoken language attitude studies (Lambert, Hodgson, Gardner, and Fillenbaum, 1960) to examine the language attitudes of prospective teachers of the deaf. A study that looks specifically at attitudes toward the outcomes of language contact in the deaf community was done by Kannapell (1985). The overall goal of the study was an examination of deaf college students' attitudes toward ASL and English. Major components of the study included a self-evaluation by the students of their language skills, including so-called Pidgin Sign English, and a self-classification of linguistic skills as ASL monolinguals, ASL-dominant bilinguals, balanced bilinguals, English-dominant bilinguals, English monolinguals, and semilinguals. In addition to the data collected in questionnaires from 205 subjects, videotaped interviews were conducted with 16 of the subjects. Kannapell observes that the subjects were more forthcoming in the interviews about their language attitudes than in the questionnaires. The interviews revealed that subjects seemed to have good information about the differences among ASL, PSE, and MCE:

> They know that there are two separate languages, ASL and English, but they still have misconceptions about ASL, for example, the view of ASL as broken or bad English. Most of these students easily associate ASL users with those who come from Deaf families and Deaf schools, but their responses to PSE users are widely varied. They associate MCE users mostly with hearing people who are learning sign language and teachers who try to teach deaf children proper English. Moreover, they still associate these sign systems with their own preconceived notions about the status of people who use them, that is, ASL users are less-educated deaf people, PSE users are college educated, MCE users are highly educated deaf people. [Lucas, 1989, p. 200]

Kannapell's study also has relevance for the fifth focus, definitions and measurement of bilingualism, in the students' self-classification. It is clear that, given the nature of the circumstances, the term *bilingual* as conventionally applied to spoken language situations may require some modification when sign language situations are taken into account. As we mentioned before, deaf bilinguals may have a command of ASL and of written English, but may choose not to *speak* English. In fact, Kannapell first raised the issue of the meaning of bilingualism for the deaf community in 1974, and stated:

> The definition of a bilingual also applies to deaf persons. Ideally the deaf adult is a fluent signer of ASL and able to read and write the English language. He will use what he feels most comfortable with. When he talks with deaf friends, he will use ASL. When he talks with hearing people, he writes English on paper, or speaks through an interpreter, or uses his speech if it is intelligible enough. [p. 11]

Other researchers have investigated and proposed ways of measuring the bilingual competencies of deaf students (i.e., Hatfield, Caccamise, and Siple, 1978; Hatfield, 1982) and others have explored the issue of bilingualism in the deaf community from a psycholinguistic perspective (e.g., Herbert, 1982; Kettrick, 1986; and Corina and Vaid, 1986).

We see, then, that the five major foci of language contact studies in spoken language situations have also been attended to in studies of the American deaf community. Having provided an overview of language contact research in the deaf community, we will now bring our attention back to the first focus, the linguistic outcomes of language contact.

The Linguistic Outcomes of Language Contact

The main focus of this book will be on the linguistic outcomes of language contact in the American deaf community. However, while our discussion will concentrate on linguistic outcomes, we will of necessity make reference to the other four foci. We will first present a model of the linguistic outcomes of language contact in the deaf community and then describe our project, the original goal of which was to analyze one particular outcome of language contact.

Linguistic outcomes that have been described for spoken language situations include lexical borrowing of different kinds (loanwords, loanblends, loan shifts, loan translations, nonce borrowing), code switching, code mixing, interference, foreigner talk, pidgins, creoles, convergence, and mixed systems). A good point of departure for discussing language contact in the deaf community is to consider what each of these outcomes would look like were they to occur in a sign language situation. Table 3 presents a model of the linguistic outcomes of language contact in the deaf community.

We see immediately that before the individual phenomena can be discussed, a fundamental distinction must be made. The distinction is between a situation involving contact between two sign languages and a situation involving a sign language and a spoken language. This distinction is necessary simply because of the difference in modality between sign languages and spoken languages. That is, the basic structural units are of necessity fundamentally very different: morphemes composed of sounds articulated in specific manners and places in the vocal tract, and morphemes composed of parts articulated by the hands, face, and body. This is

TABLE 3
Outcomes of Language Contact in the Deaf Community

Between two sign languages	Between a sign language and a spoken language	
Lexical borrowing	Following Spoken Language Criteria literally	Unique Phenomena
Foreigner talk		
Interference		Fingerspelling
Pidgins, creoles, and mixed systems	Code switching	Fingerspelling/sign combination
	Lexical borrowing	Mouthing
		CODA-Speak
		TTY conversations
		Code switching
		Contact signing (code mixing)

not to say that spoken language morphemes never include the hands, face, or body or, conversely, that sign language morphemes never include verbal articulation. But the basic structure is different. Hence, the kind of contact phenomena that result from the contact between two sign languages, both in a visual–manual modality, differ from those that result from the contact between a spoken language and a sign language, one in the oral–aural modality and one in the visual–manual modality, and it would seem necessary to consider these situations separately. Naturally, the situation is not entirely straightforward, as two sign languages may be in contact, both of which may incorporate outcomes of contact with their respective spoken languages, which may then play a role in their own contact. For example, the Italian Sign Language (LIS) sign NEVER is a lexicalized fingerspelled sign from the spoken Italian word *mai*. The handshape of the sign is I, representative of the last letter of the written Italian word. American ASL users in contact with LIS users may learn and use this sign and use it in conversation with ASL–LIS bilinguals. It is the result of spoken–sign contact and gets used in sign–sign contact situations. We will provide examples of this later in our discussion. For now, we will consider the outcomes of contact between two sign languages. It is important to notice that what we are presenting is a model.[3] While we can provide some anecdotal examples, there is as yet limited empirical research on some of the phenomena we discuss. In fact, it is interesting to notice that the bulk of language contact research in deaf communities to date has focused on the outcome of contact between spoken languages and sign languages. This may be due to at least three interrelated factors: (1) the relationship between the spoken language and the sign language in the deaf community and their relative functions, particularly in the area of education, (2) limited knowledge about the linguistic structure of the sign language, and (3) doubts as to the status of the sign language as a "real language." It is our hope that our model may encourage researchers to explore the outcomes of contact between two sign languages.

Contact between Two Sign Languages

In studies of spoken language contact, lexical borrowing refers to the occurrence of a lexical item from one language in another language, and the borrowed item can be more or less integrated into the phonological, morphological, and syntactic systems of the borrowing language. Phonological and morphological integration means that some change in the original form takes place. In American English, words such as *croissant* or *spaghetti* are phonologically integrated: their phonetic realization in American English is different than it is in French or Italian. Such cases are called *loanwords* by some researchers. However, integration may only be of a partial nature. Haugen (1953; described in Romaine, 1989, p. 58) proposed three stages in the process of phonological adaptation: (1) the bilingual introduces the new word in a phonetic form which is as close to that of the model as possible; (2) as other speakers start using it, it may be integrated, and native elements will be substituted for foreign ones; (3) it will be used by monolinguals unaware of the foreign origin of the world.

Loanwords can be integrated at the morphological level in vari-

---

3. The model for the structure of ASL signs themselves that we use is the one developed by Scott K. Liddell and Robert E. Johnson. In this model, signs are seen as composed of sequentially produced movement and hold segments, the segments in turn composed of bundles of articulatory features such as handshape, location, orientation, and non-manual signals. (See Liddell and Johnson, 1989.)

ous ways as well. The morphology of the recipient language has traditionally been seen as more resistant to integration, but as Romaine (1989) points out, "The potential for morphological transference, however, is almost always present in bilinguals by virtue of the fact that when speakers borrow words from one language into another, they may cause the morphology of the recipient language to be realigned through the introduction of foreign morphemes" (p. 59). Traditionally, some degree of phonological integration has been a major criterion, along with degree of acceptance and use, in distinguishing borrowing from code switching, that is, the occurrence of an item (or items) without integration. As Romaine reports, Poplack, Sankoff, and Miller (1988) in their description of French–English contact in Ottawa/Hull, distinguished between "established loanwords" and "nonce borrowings": "Nonce borrowings are integrated only momentarily and occur infrequently" (Romaine, 1989, p. 61). However, they also found examples of unintegrated English morphemes occurring with French participial and verbal affixes, and Romaine observes that "For any given word in bilingual discourse which appears to be a loanword, it is often difficult to decide whether it represents code-switching" (p. 61). A vivid example of this was provided recently in a television interview with Warren Cromartie, an American who has played baseball in Japan for several years and has learned Japanese. In reporting a conversation with his Japanese teammates to the English-speaking reporter, he spoke two or three words of Japanese, then switched to English but produced it with what could be described as the accent of a Japanese person speaking English. This is an intriguing example because lexically, morphologically, and syntactically, he was speaking English and the event could be considered an instance of code switching. Phonologically, however, it was not entirely English, so the switch might not be considered complete. It would seem to be a case of a switch as opposed to a borrowing, though, on the grounds that it was at least two sentences in length, as opposed to being a single lexical item.

A description of lexical borrowing between two sign languages presents similar definition problems. It is clear that the signs from one sign language occur in other sign languages, and the characterization of such occurrences as borrowing or as code switching might seem straightforward, but it is not. Let us consider some examples of borrowing. In recent years, the ASL signs for a variety of countries—ITALY, CHINA, JAPAN, SWEDEN, GERMANY— have begun to be replaced with the signs for those countries actually used in the countries in question. That is, the ASL sign for ITALY is starting to be replaced with the Italian sign for ITALY. (See Fig. 1). In a first analysis, one might say that this is a straightforward case of borrowing: a lexical item from one sign language becomes part of the lexicon of another and is phonologically and morphologically integrated into the recipient sign language. The difficulty is with the term *phonologically integrated*. The Italian sign has a particular segmental structure, handshape, palm orientation, and location. It happens that ASL has at its disposal the same segmental structure, handshape, palm orientation, and location. If an ASL signer sees and learns and exactly reproduces the Italian sign and uses it in ASL discourse, it would seem that an entire lexical item is being borrowed but that we cannot really talk of phonological integration in this case. The two sign languages share identical components in this case, so there is no integration into ASL phonology to speak of, in the same way that the spoken French word

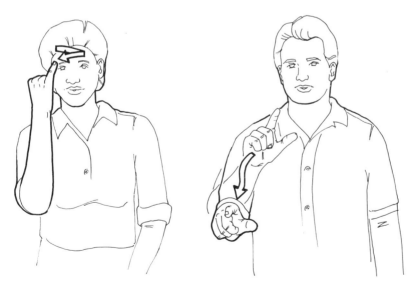

Figure 1 Drawings of (left) ITALY (American Sign Language) and (right) ITALY (Italian Sign Language).

croissant is integrated into American English phonology with a phonological result that is quite different from the original. The criterion of phonological integration in defining lexical borrowing in sign languages, then, may not always apply.

In the case of this particular sign, it would seem that ASL has the same components but not in the same combination or with the same meaning as they have in LIS (Lingua Italiana dei Segni, or Italian Sign Language). For example, that particular combination of components in ASL might have the function of a classifier predicate used to describe the shape of a particular object. On the other hand, because the Italian sign is becoming widely used and accepted by ASL users who may not know its origin and simply learn it as "the sign for Italy," we cannot say that the occurrence of this sign is simply a case of code switching, that is, that a bilingual ASL user inserts an element of LIS in his otherwise ASL discourse.

Not that cases of phonological integration do not exist. There may be cases where one sign language uses handshapes, locations, palm orientations, and segmental structure not found in ASL and, in the course of borrowing, some or all of those elements adapt to the constraints of ASL phonology. An example may be provided from studies comparing French Sign Language and ASL, two historically related sign languages. Many signs which are made at the elbow in Langue des Signes Française (LSF) have slowly shifted location in ASL so that they are made on the hands (De Santis, 1977). This is the result of change over time, but such historical evidence might lead to the hypothesis that the hand is a preferable location to the elbow in ASL and that foreign signs produced at the elbow and borrowed into ASL might eventually be produced on the hands.

Characterizing borrowing between two sign languages in terms of phonological integration, then, may not always be possible. This may be due to the fundamental nature of sign language phonologies, each of which is composed of many more basic components than spoken language phonologies and each of which shares many of these components with other sign languages. Bob Johnson (personal communication, 1991) has observed that pure minimal pairs of the kind used to demonstrate contrast in spoken languages are hard to find in ASL and that this may be so because there are so many more basic components from which to build contrastive units—so many handshapes, locations, palm orientations, and facial expressions—as opposed to the relatively limited number of components available in spoken languages. The corollary of this for contact phenomena is that sign languages may share many of the same components and each may have a relatively small number of unique features, if any, so that "borrowing" between sign languages means either producing a combination of components that already exists in the recipient language and learning the meaning given to that combination in the original sign language, or combining the components that one already has at one's disposal in a new way.

In either case, the components themselves may not necessarily change their form from one sign language to another in the same way that spoken language forms change as they are borrowed from one spoken language phonology into another spoken language phonology. In this sense, phonological integration may not mean a *change* in the forms. It may refer to a degree of similarity between the phonological systems of two languages such that a form from one language can be immediately integrated into another. It is considered a borrowing because it clearly originates in another system, but the process of entry into the new system does not include change in phonological shape. An analogy in spoken languages would be borrowing between two languages whose phonologies share many of the same features. For example, the borrowing of the Italian words *ciao* and *pizza* into Spanish may not involve any phonological integration, since the two languages are almost identical as far as those lexical items are concerned. However, the same two languages may be very different in other parts of their respective phonologies. Were a Venezuelan speaker of Spanish to borrow the Italian word *vermicelli*, the difference between the two phonologies might reveal itself, were the phonetic realization to be [bɛrmisɛ́li]. A further difference between the *ciao* and *pizza* case between Spanish and Italian and sign language cases is this: With *ciao* and *pizza*, there may be no phonological integration to speak of and also no change in the meaning of the words—they may mean the same thing and be used the same way in both languages [although Grosjean (personal communication) observes that no two languages have exactly the same phonological structure, that there will always be some phonological adaptation, and that a borrowing never means exactly the same thing in the host language and the guest language]. Between sign languages, as in the ITALY case, there may be no change of form, and so no phonological integration in the usual way the term has been used in contact studies, but a significant difference in meaning. The form either may not exist in the recipient language (although it would be a plausible form and its component parts do exist) or it may exist with an unrelated meaning. An analogy with spoken languages might be the case in which a form is borrowed which already exists in the language with a different meaning, resulting in the creation of homonyms. An example might be borrowing the Italian word *ciao* into English, which already has the form *chow* (itself of course also a borrowing from Chinese, albeit an earlier one than *ciao*). A speaker of American English must learn that the same phonetic form [čau] now has two meanings. Table 4 summarizes the similarities and differences between sign and spoken lexical borrowing.

The same issues arise for instances of loanblends and nonce borrowings. Haugen (1950) defines loanblends as cases in which one part of a word is borrowed and the other part belongs to the original language, as in the example reported by Clyne (1967) of German spoken in Australia: *gumbaum, gum* being English and *baum* being German, meaning "gumtree." Another example was

TABLE 4
Comparison of Lexical Borrowing in Spoken and Signed Languages

Phonological integration[a]	Change in meaning	Spoken language	Signed language (ASL)
√	—	Italian → English *pizza*	CLUB
—	—	Italian → Spanish *ciao*	CHINA
—	√	English: *ciao/chow*	ITALY and classifier predicate with same phonological shape
√	√	Not necessary or possible: With phonological integration, any potential meaning conflict with identical forms is resolved.	

[a](from original to recipient language)

provided recently in the Washington Post (August 3, 1991): *zaitech*, a term used in Japan which is a combination of the Japanese word meaning "assets" and a portion of the English word "technology." The term means the manipulation of stocks, real estate, rare art works, and other financial assets in highly technical ways to enhance profit. We can imagine a case in which a compound sign was composed of an ASL and a foreign sign but, again, if the foreign sign is composed of components that already exist in ASL, the same arguments we made previously apply. Furthermore, the phonological structure of sign languages allows a unique kind of simultaneous blending, as attested in the sign HOW, which has the location, palm orientation, and segmental structure of the ASL sign HOW, but the handshape of the BSL sign HOW. This is different from the necessarily sequential combination of elements from two spoken languages.

As we mentioned earlier, the term *nonce borrowing* was introduced by Sankoff and Poplack (1986) to account for single lexical items which are syntactically and morphologically but not always phonologically integrated into the recipient language. As Romaine (1989) explains, "Nonce words differ from established loanwords only quantitatively with respect to frequency of use, degree of acceptance, level of phonological integration . . . " (p. 142). Again, we can imagine cases in which signs from other sign languages might behave like nonce borrowings, but the nature of phonological integration would still be an issue.

Somewhat less troublesome are loan shifts and loan translations. For spoken languages, a loan shift "consists of taking a word in the base language and extending its meaning so that it corresponds to that of a word in the other language" (Romaine, 1989, p. 55). This is also referred to as semantic extension, and classic examples include the Portugese word *grossería* ("rude remark") which has come to mean "grocery" for Portugese–English bilinguals living in the United States (Pap, 1949), or Italian *fattoria* ("farm") which has come to mean "factory" for many Italian–Americans. It is important to notice that these are changes in the original language as a result of contact with English, not additions to English. An example of a loan translation or calque in spoken languages is the case of English *skyscraper* which occurs in French as *gratteciel* ("scrape + sky") and in Italian and Spanish as *grattacielo* and *rascacielos*, respectively. Again, we can imagine both loan shifts and loan translations occurring as a result of contact between sign languages, and such examples are easier to account for in the terms used for spoken languages since they would involve the use of whole lexical items or the extension of meaning with no change in form.

Studies of spoken language contact traditionally draw distinctions among lexical borrowing, code switching, and code mixing. While lexical borrowing is understood to include some kind of integration of the item into the recipient language, along with widespread use and acceptance, the terms *code switching* and *code mixing* are generally understood to mean a complete switch to another language without integration into the recipient language. Some researchers distinguish between the two phenomena, characterizing code mixing as switching that takes place *intrasententially*—within the boundaries of a sentence—as opposed to code switching, which takes place *intersententially*—across the boundaries of sentences (Bokamba, 1985; Kachru, 1978; Sridhar and Sridhar, 1980; Thelander, 1976). A great deal of attention has been given to defining the precise constraints on code switching and code mixing in spoken languages, that is, at which precise points switching is allowed, what kinds of items are candidates for switching, and so forth. However, while we will discuss code switching and code mixing when we consider the outcomes of contact between a sign language and a spoken language, we know of no studies as yet that look at code switching and code mixing between two sign languages. It is not hard to imagine either case, however—a bilingual signer of ASL and Langue des Signes Québecoise (LSQ, the sign language used in Québec, distinct from ASL) could be conversing with another bilingual signer and either switch from ASL to LSQ or mix elements from LSQ into his ASL discourse or vice versa; a bilingual signer of ASL and LIS switches or mixes between the two languages, and so forth. This is an area that will clearly yield some very interesting data when research attention is focused upon it, and interesting questions will come up. For example, can any constraints on switching and mixing be identified; are certain lexical categories more prone to switching and mixing than others; do switching and mixing have the same kinds of discourse functions that they have in spoken languages, etc. And again, the role of phonological integration in distinguishing among borrowing, switching, and mixing will have to be considered in understanding these events as they occur in sign languages.

We can also imagine cases in the contact between two sign languages of interference, as distinct from other contact phenomena. Many definitions of interference have been proposed but many of the definitions do not adequately distinguish interference from code switching or borrowing (see, for example, Weinreich, 1968; Haugen, 1956; Mackey, 1968; Clyne, 1972). One useful definition is that offered by Grosjean (1982): " . . . interference [is] the involuntary influence of one language on the other. This type of influence becomes quite apparent when a bilingual is speaking to a monolingual. In this situation the bilingual realizes that code switching and borrowing might impede communication. If, despite this, one language is influenced by the other, one can then talk of interference" (p. 299). However, as Romaine (1989) points out, part of the difficulty in distinguishing between interference and other contact phenomena is that "they must be dealt with at the level of the individual as well as the community" (p. 50). That is, what begins as "sporadic and idiosyncratic" interference in the individual speaker may become the norm at the community level, over time. Again, we know of no systematic studies of interference between two sign languages but we can easily imagine cases of interference. In fact, where phonological integration might not be a useful criterion for defining instances of borrowing between sign languages, it might be precisely the lack of phonological integration that might signal interference—for example, the involuntary use of a handshape, location, palm orientation, movement, or facial expression from one sign language in the discourse of another. Signers are said to have "accents" when they use sign languages other than their own, and we suggest that these "accents" are examples of a lack of complete phonological integration, of what Grosjean refers to as "static interference," mentioned earlier. We should note that lack of phonological integration might not always be a reliable indicator, as a signer might use a form that exists in both sign languages, simply with a different meaning in both. We also suggest that interference may not be restricted to phonology and may occur in the morphological and syntactic components as well, and empirical studies are needed to explore the occurrence of interference at all levels.

Another outcome of language contact is foreigner talk, first explored in spoken languages by Ferguson (1971; 1975) and Ferguson and De Bose (1977). Features of foreigner talk for spoken languages proposed by Ferguson and De Bose include slow exaggerated speech, greater loudness, increased repetition, full forms instead of contractions, increased use of standard forms, replacements, reduction of inflection, and greater use of feedback devices. Myles-Zitzer (1990) examined the linguistic and nonlinguistic accommodations made by native Deaf signers to nonnative hearing second-language learners of ASL with varying proficiencies in ASL and modified Ferguson and De Bose's inventory to include slow exaggerated signs, larger and wider signs, increased repetition, full forms instead of contractions, increased use of standard forms, replacements, reduction of inflection, and greater use of feedback devices. Cokely (1983) also uses the term *foreigner talk* in his discussion of the outcomes of language contact in the deaf community. However, both researchers are focusing on the interaction of hearing and deaf signers, as opposed to the interaction of native signers of different sign languages, and Myles-Zitzer (1990) equates foreigner talk with PSE: "It can thus be argued that the Pidgin Sign English which emerges may be viewed as a product of the linguistic accommodations between Deaf and hearing individuals which are necessitated by the need to effectively communicate" (p. 60). The difficulty with this equation is that foreigner talk does include elements of the nonnative speaker's first language.

Consider an analogy from spoken language contact situations. In the contact between a native speaker of Italian, for example, and a nonnative speaker, it would be strange to expect that the foreigner-talk variety of Italian used by the native speaker would include any elements of the nonnative speaker's first language. More likely, the foreigner-talk variety of Italian would simply be a modified version of Italian, incorporating some or all of the features proposed by Ferguson and De Bose. But Myles-Zitzer's equating foreigner talk with PSE implies that ASL foreigner talk includes English features. As we will see, there does exist a kind of signing that fits this description, but we will not call it foreigner talk. And again, to our knowledge there exist no empirical studies of the foreigner talk resulting from the interaction of native signers of different sign languages, although this would be an extremely interesting area to explore, with plenty of occasions upon which to collect data, as deaf people from all over the world increasingly come in contact with each other. The same is true for contact phenomena such as pidgins, creoles, convergence, and mixed systems.

As we will discuss at length, one outcome of language contact in the deaf community has been labeled a pidgin, but it concerns the contact between a spoken language and a sign language. Whether the sociolinguistic circumstances that gave rise to spoken language pidgins and the linguistic outcomes that we call pidgins have parallels in the deaf community is a topic for future research. We can speculate briefly as to how a sign language pidgin might come about and what it might look like, by drawing an analogy to the sociolinguistic circumstances that have typically given rise to spoken language pidgins (with recognition of the fact that there is significant disagreement among pidgin and creole scholars as to the linguistic and sociolinguistic natures of these languages.) Say, for example, that the native signers of two mutually unintelligible sign languages are in contact with each other, and that their mutual goal is to learn a third sign language, for reasons of upward social mobility and survival. They are adult users of their respective languages and they are removed from contact with their respective languages. In addition, access to native users of the target sign language is restricted and they end up learning it from each other. Finally, they find themselves in oppressed social and economic circumstances.

It would seem that these would be the conditions necessary for the emergence of a language analogous to spoken language pidgins. As we will discuss, the language that has been labeled a pidgin in the deaf community does not fit these conditions nor are the linguistic features of what emerges analogous to those of spoken language pidgins. Not that these conditions have never existed or have never given rise to a sign language pidgin. They simply have yet to be documented.

Likewise for convergence and mixed systems, as described for spoken languages by Gumperz and Wilson (1971). We will describe what appears to be a mixed system, but it is the result of the contact between a spoken language and a sign language, not between two sign languages. There is no reason why two independent sign languages which have coexisted for a long period of time should not have evolved a third, converged system, in the way that some spoken languages have, and such a situation may exist. It simply has yet to be documented, to our knowledge. Some researchers have made the suggestion that ASL itself is a creole or the result of a creolization process (see Fischer, 1978, for example) in the sense that children acquired as their first language in residential school settings the result of contact between French Sign Language and the ASL in use in the United States at the time it came in contact with French Sign Language. We would suggest that while there was clearly *language contact* between French Sign Language and ASL, it is not clear that the sociolinguistic circumstances were exactly analogous to those in spoken language situations in which pidgins and creoles come about. We will elaborate upon this in Chapter 2.

This, then, is our account of contact phenomena that may occur between two sign languages. Our account has been based upon phenomena that occur in spoken language situations, but there may be some outcomes that are unique to the deaf community that at this point are evidenced only anecdotally. For example, there is anecdotal evidence that one linguistic outcome of large gatherings of deaf people from all over the world, such as the World Federation of the Deaf or the Deaf Way conference held in Washington, D.C., in 1989 (with over 5700 people in attendance), is the fairly rapid emergence of what could be called a lingua franca, say, within 2 or 3 days. One can speculate as to whether this has to do with the similarity among sign language structures and whether spoken lingua francas emerge at a similar rate. These sign lingua francas are apparently distinct from the International Sign Language that is being learned and used by interpreters and presenters, for example, for international events, but the precise nature of structural similarities and differences is yet not documented (Moody, 1989). It would also be very interesting to understand some of the processes whereby these lingua francas are formed—how are lexical items negotiated and decided upon, for example. Discussion of the lingua francas in deaf contact situations is also somewhat ironic, because probably the most common question asked by hearing laymen about sign language is whether or not sign language is universal. The answer, of course, is no, that all sign languages are unique and most are mutually unintelligible, but one cannot help but wonder if it is precisely the fact that sign languages do indeed have many structural similarities (which is different from saying that sign language is universal) that allows for the apparently rapid formation of lingua francas. However, we will hide behind a hedge: It may not be that the rate of formation is any faster than that for spoken languages. It may be simply that the formation of sign language lingua francas has not yet been described and that its description will provide insight into the formation of spoken language ones as well.

We will turn our attention now to the outcomes of contact between a sign language and a spoken language.

Contact Between a Sign Language and a Spoken Language

Following spoken language criteria literally

Figure 1 shows that considering the contact between a sign language and a spoken language requires a further breakdown, that is, what the outcomes of contact look like if one follows spoken language criteria literally and what the unique outcomes of contact are. Again, this distinction is necessary because of the difference in modalities. We want to point out that, as we learn more about different deaf communities around the world, the model we present here may change. For example, we are beginning to know more about communities such as the Yucatec Maya one in the Yucatan Peninsula, in which all members of the community, both hearing and deaf, sign (Johnson, 1991). This is of course reminiscent of Martha's Vineyard, and reports of other such communities are beginning to surface, for example, in Venezuela (Pietrosemoli, personal communication). Not only are these communities in which everyone signs, but in the Yucatec case, neither language is written. As R. E. Johnson (personal communication) observes, the bulk of language contact research concerns contact between languages at least one of which has a written form, and that is the case in the contact between ASL and English. It is not clear what the outcomes of language contact are, if any, in communities in which everyone signs and in which none of the languages in contact has a written form.

If we consider the outcomes of contact between a sign language and a spoken language literally in terms of spoken language criteria, a description of code switching, for example, means that the person literally stops signing and starts speaking, at a sentence boundary. A literal interpretation of code mixing means that, within a sentence boundary, the person stops signing and speaks an English word or words, and then resumes signing, or vice versa—stops speaking English, signs one or more signs, and then resumes speaking English. There exists abundant anecdotal evidence that both of these situations occur. For example, hearing bilinguals may produce ASL sentences or signs with each other (with no deaf people present) in the course of spoken English conversations—we can easily imagine the following English sentence: " And when he told me about it, my mouth went like this: (switch to sign for JAW DROP OPEN)". Deaf bilinguals may speak English words or sentences in the course of ASL conversations with each other or with hearing bilinguals—during a conversation in a restaurant concerning how the bill was going to be paid, a deaf acquaintance of ours switched from ASL to English and mouthed "Have cash" and then went immediately back to ASL. Hearing bilinguals may speak English words or sentences (*not* accompanied by signs) with deaf bilinguals in the course of an ASL conversation—we can recall situations in which a hearing interlocutor mouthed without voice "What?!" in response to shocking news presented in ASL.

Likewise, instances of lexical borrowing that follow literal spoken language criteria may occur. Battison (1978) talks about cases "in which an existing ASL sign takes on the semantic properties of one of its English glosses," and calls these cases loan translations. He gives the following example: "There is a sign LOOK-FOR/SEEK/ SEARCH which is often redundantly followed by the unrelated FOR when signing in English, to render the English phrase 'look for'—that is, the sign LOOK-FOR is reanalyzed as meaning 'look'." We suggest that this is more aptly described as a case of loan shift, meaning that the original meaning of the sign has been extended or changed in some way. The actual form of the sign has not changed.[4] Another example comes from our data and involves the sign GROW. There are at least two signs that can be glossed as GROW, one used in the context of talking about children and the other in the context of talking about plants. As an apparent result of contact with English, however, the latter has come to be used in conjunction with the fingerspelled sign #UP, to talk about children

4. The irony with this particular sign, of course, is that it most likely began its life as an initialized French sign, the C handshape representing the first letter of the written French word *chercher*.

growing up. We argue that this is a case of loan shift, as the form of the sign has not changed but the meaning has been extended. There are cases of loan translation and Battison provides a good one, with the sign STAND, which has come to be used in the collocation CAN'T STAND. This is a direct translation into ASL of an English collocation. Other examples include compounds such as BOY-FRIEND, GIRLFRIEND, HOMEWORK, HOMESICK, and BLACK-BOARD. Loan translations also occur in English, when hearing bilinguals form spoken English morphemes from the mouth configuration that is part of an ASL sign. For example, the mouth configuration that is part of the classifier predicate meaning LARGE PILE OF PAPERS or THICK BOOK—a mouth configuration having an adverbial meaning of LARGE QUANTITY or THICK ENTITY—can be glossed as "cha," phonetically [ča]. Hearing bilingual graduate students have been known to produce this sentence in spoken English: "I have cha homework."

Another example was provided to us by one of our colleagues who formed the English verb "speesh" from the mouth configuration of the sign that can be glossed as WELL-I'LL-BE-DARNED, and said "Well, speesh me!" This sentence was spoken in English to hearing bilinguals, with no deaf people present. The sentence structure itself might not be accepted by native English speakers as English and may itself be the product of a bilingual environment, and it is important to note that these usages are not widespread—they do not technically meet the criteria of frequency and acceptance that traditionally define lexical borrowing. However, just their occurrence indicates the potential for this kind of loan translation from ASL to English.

So we see that there are contact outcomes in the deaf community that can be described following spoken language criteria. However, there are also some unique phenomena, to which we now turn our attention.

Unique Phenomena

Before we discuss specific examples of unique phenomena, it is necessary to clarify why we consider these unique. This brings us back to the debate about the terms used to define contact phenomena and is related to our discussion of phonological integration. Borrowing, for example, has been defined in terms of spoken language contact and generally refers to the relationship between two spoken language phonologies and morphologies. The basic premise is that spoken language phonologies, while unique, are composed of the same basic parts—the sounds articulated by the vocal tract—and that borrowing takes place within the same modality. When a work of spoken Italian is borrowed into American English, that means that an Italian phonological event enters the American English phonological system and may undergo some changes. But the basic parts of language in question are the same: sounds. A lexical item that was at one time part of Italian becomes part of English. On the other hand, contact between a sign language and a spoken language necessarily involves two modalities, and the outcomes of contact need to be defined in different ways as a result. We suggest that the terms that have been used to define spoken language contact phenomena, such as borrowing, cannot be indiscriminately applied to sign-spoken events. The best example we can provide concerns fingerspelling.[5]

Fingerspelling has traditionally been given as an example of lexical borrowing from English to ASL (Battison, 1978). But we suggest that while fingerspelling is clearly an example of a relationship between English and ASL, and while that relationship is quite clearly an outcome of language contact, that relationship is not best described as borrowing. Let us consider a specific example. The orthographic representation of the English word *what* occurs as a fingerspelled lexical item in ASL, consisting of a sequence of four morphemes (W-H-A-T), what other analyses might have described as a sequence of four handshapes. Within the Liddell–Johnson framework, the handshape which is a symbol for the English orthographic letter is only *one* feature of a morpheme whose segmental structure consists of a hold and also includes information about location and orientation. In any language, morphemes are defined as the smallest meaningful units, and they may be bound or free. In ASL, what have traditionally been thought of simply as handshapes or as letters are morphemes in the standard meaning of that word: They consist of the pairing of a form with a meaning. They have the segmental structure of ASL signs, of which the handshape is one part, and they have the meaning of "signed symbol for English

5. The symbol # is conventionally used to indicate a lexicalized fingerspelled sign. Dashes are conventionally used to indicate full fingerspelling.

orthographic symbol." They are free morphemes which may also have bound allomorphs when they occur with other fingerspelled morphemes. We do not consider the morphemes that make up fingerspelled signs to be "letters" and we do not consider finger-spelling to be English. The forms used are ASL forms; fingerspelling is part of ASL (Fig. 2). In describing fingerspelling, the salient re-lationship is not between the respective phonologies of two lan-guages, as it is with spoken languages. Rather, it is between the orthographic system of one language (English) and the phonological system of another (ASL).

Furthermore, as Davis (1989) points out in his description of fingerspelling in interpreting, the relationship between the phono-logical systems of spoken languages is truly one of *borrowing*—one language *borrows* the sounds of another and the result is a *loan*. At no point, however, can the relationship between English orthog-raphy and ASL phonology be characterized as borrowing. ASL mor-phemes are never borrowed from the orthographic English event; they are simply used to *represent* the orthographic event. An ex-ample of a proper analogy from spoken languages for the relation-ship between ASL fingerspelling and English orthography is a speaker's pronunciation of the English letters used to orthograph-ically represent a Spanish word, such as [je-u-ɛn-ti-e] for *junta*. [p. 97]

Fingerspelling, then, is a unique outcome of language contact, and in fact it is not the outcome of contact between a sign language and a spoken language, but rather between a sign language and the orthographic system used to represent that spoken language. It may take different forms. It may be what we could call "full finger-spelling," in which each morpheme is clearly produced. This kind of fingerspelling occurs, for example, in situations in which names or terms are being introduced for the first time. The signer may even choose to support his arm and gaze directly at the hand producing the fingerspelling. This is different from the many examples in ASL of what we can call "lexicalized fingerspelling"—examples such as #BANK, #BACK, #SO, #DOG, and many more—in which the segmental structure has changed, handshape assimilation has taken place, location and orientation have changed, and movement may have been added, in accordance with the morpheme structure con-straints of ASL. Fingerspelling may also occur in combination with

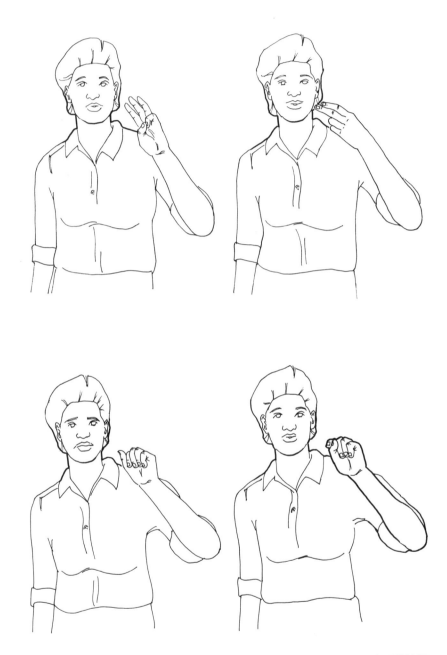

Figure 2   Drawings of W-H-A-T with full fingerspelling and (next page) #WHAT with lexicalized fingerspelling.

lexical signs, in compounds, for example, where one component is a lexical sign and the other is fingerspelling. We see an example of this in the sign LIFE#STYLE, which consists of the lexical sign LIFE and the fingerspelled sign #STYLE. This is also probably an example of a loan translation, demonstrating that several contact phenomena may interact. Kelly (1990) researched the use of fingerspelling among senior citizens in Baltimore and found examples of these combinations. She also found sign–fingerspelling–sign combinations or fingerspelling–sign combinations such as CHURCH E-P-I-S-C-O-P-A-L CHURCH, #GUESS GUESS, and EASY #TAKE IT EASY, and examples that consisted of sentence fragments and were not limited to single lexical items—for example, T-O-O-K-A-C-T-I-V-E-P-A-R-T and E-N-C-O-U-R-A-G-E-D-M-E. (Dashes indicate full fingerspelling, as opposed to the # symbol, which marks lexicalized fingerspelling.)

As we pointed out earlier, fingerspelling has been a major teaching tool in deaf education from the very beginning and in fact has been used as the *only* teaching tool in some settings. The Rochester Method, for example, requires the use of fingerspelling for all instruction, to the exclusion of signs. It is not surprising, then, that fingerspelling should play such an important role in the discourse of deaf people. Battison (1978) claims that "while ASL signers borrow and restructure fingerspelled words (making them essentially like native signs), they incorporate these loans into their in-group language (ASL) and not into their inter-group language (a Sign English pidgin). English-based restructured loans are not used in the Sign English pidgin, nor is a Sign English pidgin an outcome of using these loans" (p. 105). We will return to this claim later. Fingerspelling is often used even when a lexical sign already exists in ASL, and there exist many "doublets"—CAR and #CAR, BED and #BED, GO and #GO, for example—so it clearly has discourse functions. The precise discourse functions of fingerspelling are a topic that deserves research attention. Another situation that would be interesting to investigate is the one in which two sign languages are in contact and one borrows fingerspelling from another. We are seeing examples of this as ASL comes into contact with other sign languages that use far less fingerspelling than ASL. It is somewhat analogous to the situation that Romaine (1989) describes for the relationship between Konkani and Kannada, whereby Konkani borrows a relativization strategy from Kannada that Kannada had in turn borrowed from Indo-European, the effect being "borrowing a borrowing" (Romaine, 1989, p. 73).

Also deserving research attention is the nature of fingerspelling in other sign languages, particularly those in which the writing system of the spoken language in question is other than the Roman alphabet. There is some evidence from research. For example, in describing Taiwan Sign Language (TSL), Smith (1989) states that "TSL has no kind of fingerspelling. When specific characters are being discussed, they are either written out on paper or on the palm of the weak hand, either with a pen or simply by tracing the character with the index finger" (pp. 3–4). The fingerspelling alphabet used by Russian deaf people reflects in part the Cyrillic writing system (Gerankina, 1972) and we have anecdotal reports of manual representations of Hebrew and Arabic by deaf people in contact with those languages. We also know anecdotally of diacritics being represented, as in the fingerspelling used for Yugoslav names in Trieste, in which the diacritic ˘ on the letter č is represented. This is clearly a very fruitful area for future investigations.

Another unique outcome of the contact between a sign language and a spoken language is mouthing. The first distinction that must be made concerns the difference between mouth configurations that are integral parts of ASL lexical items and that have no relationship whatsoever with English lexical items and mouth configurations that can be traced to English lexical items. Examples of the former include the CHA example discussed earlier, along with the mouth configurations that are part of signs such as NOT-YET, FINALLY (PAH), ADMIT, and BEAT (see Fig. 3). The latter do have a clear relationship with spoken English. Davis (1989) proposes a range of mouthing, from "English mouthing" (the clear and full articulation of an English word, without voice) to "reduced English mouthing" (where only a portion of the articulation of the English word is preserved), to ASL mouthing, described above. Examples of reduced mouthing include the mouth configuration in the signs FINISH or HAVE (Davis, 1989). The mouth configuration in these signs is related to the English word but is lexicalized at this point and is an integral part of the ASL lexical item. As such, its relation to English may not necessarily be recognized by ASL signers. Other instances of reduced mouthing, as we will see, are not lexicalized. Both full and reduced mouthing are clearly outcomes of ASL–English contact and, as we mentioned earlier, may even occur without signing. And it is important to understand that while both

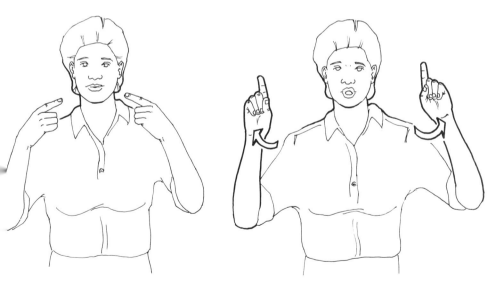

Figure 3   FINALLY with American Sign Language configuration.

mouthing and spoken English may be used in contact situations, they are distinct events.

A third unique phenomenon is the code switching which occurs when a signer stops signing ASL and switches to one of the manual codes invented to represent English, such as SEE I. We include this in the group of unique phenomena and not with the outcomes of contact between two sign languages precisely because the manual code is devised to manually represent a spoken language. The spoken language is central to its invention. Another reason that it belongs in this group is that this code switching often includes the use of audible spoken English.

A fourth outcome is a phenomenon that has recently come to our attention anecdotally, known as "CODA-speak" (J. Schuchman, personal communication; Jacobs, 1992). CODA is the acronym often used to identify the hearing children of deaf adults, individuals who often have ASL as their native language. While there is as yet no empirical research on this phenomenon, anecdotal evidence indicates that CODA-speak consists of spoken English words produced with ASL syntactic structure, what might be called "spoken ASL." It has not been formally described as of this writing, so we cannot say what its English morphological and prosodic features might be. However, it probably also occurs with the hearing children of deaf people in other countries and is clearly a contact outcome unique to spoken language–sign language bilinguals. A fifth, similar outcome is the English typed during TTY (teletypewriter) conversations, which often displays features of ASL (Mather, 1991).

A fifth unique outcome of language contact in the American deaf community is what we have called contact signing, a kind of signing that incorporates features of ASL and English and may include other phenomena we have described such as loan translations, fingerspelling, and mouthing. It was the goal of our project to describe the linguistic and sociolinguistic features of contact signing and to reexamine claims that it is a pidgin. We turn our attention now to that description and reexamination.

Taking Another Look at Language Contact in the Deaf Community

Getting It on Tape

Before describing the details of our data collection methodology, we will begin with a brief overview of the whole project. As we said earlier, the ultimate goals of the project were to look at the linguistic and sociolinguistic features of contact signing and to reexamine claims that it is a pidgin and the result of deaf–hearing interaction. Having implemented a data-collection methodology designed to elicit contact signing, the specific segments of the videotaped data to be analyzed were selected with the assistance of native signer judges. This judgment process was an integral part of the project and produced some unexpected findings which we will report. Following the judgment process, the linguistic features of the selected segments were analyzed and the results of that analysis, along with the transcripts of the segments, are presented here.

We will now turn to a description of our data collection methodology. A serious problem with earlier descriptions of language contact phenomena in the American deaf community concerns precisely the lack of data or the inadequacy of the data used to support claims about the linguistic features of the signing being described. For example, neither in Woodward (1973b) nor in Woodward and Markowicz (1975) is there any description of the sample that served as the source for the list of features proposed for PSE. J. C. Woodward (personal communication) has indicated that the description of PSE was based in part on a sample from his dissertation research: 140 individuals, ranging in age from 13 to 55, with 9 black signers and 131 white signers. But these data still present a problem because they were elicited by a hearing researcher on a one-on-one basis with the use of a questionnaire and they were not interactional, and the signers involved range from Deaf native ASL signers to hearing nonnative signers, making it virtually impossible to separate out features of the language produced that are a function of language variation from the features that are a function of second-language learning. For example, Woodward and Markowicz (1975, p. 18) claim that the ASL rule of negative incorporation can occur in PSE but that "deaf signers use more negative incorporation than hearing signers." This may indeed be true, but it might also reflect a difference in language competence (i.e., native signers knowing and competently using a rule that non-native signers may be in the process of learning) rather than reflecting language contact between hearing and deaf signers.

As we have suggested from our description of the participants in language contact situations in the deaf community, it would seem that deaf language production and hearing language production are necessarily different by virtue of differences in language learning backgrounds. Furthermore, the features of contact signing (what other researchers refer to as PSE) cannot be described based on data that not only combine native and nonnative signers' productions but also are not interactional.

Researchers have certainly been aware of the need to separate native production from non-native production. Lee (1982, p. 131) reports that

W. C. Stokoe (personal communication) suggests that there may in fact be two PSE continua: a PSEd produced by deaf signers and a PSEh produced by hearing signers. PSEd is likely to have more ASL grammatical structures and to omit English inflections. PSEh tends to have greater English influence and rarely approaches the ASL extreme of the continuum.

So the need for separation of data sources has been recognized but not reflected in the actual descriptions of PSE that have been produced. For example, Reilly and McIntire (1980) base their description of the differences between PSE and ASL on videotapes of a children's story signed by four informants. Three of the informants are hearing, three have deaf parents, and two of the three hearing informants did not use ASL as children. The instructions used to elicit different versions of the story were given either in ASL or, as Reilly and McIntire (1980, p. 155) report, "in PSE and spoken English simultaneously . . . or interpreted, i.e., signed as they were being read aloud by the investigator." In their conclusions, the researchers (1980, p. 183) state:

> It seems that there is a gradation from structures that are more obvious to the language learner (classifiers and directional verbs) to those that are more and more subtle (sustained signs and facial and other non-manual behaviors). This gradation is reflected in differential usage by different signers.

Once again, we see the "apples and oranges" problem resulting from descriptions of contact phenomena based on the signing of signers with different levels of competence and ages of acquisition. Data collection in analogous spoken language situations does not typically yield naturalistic data. Similarly, it is not clear that the data upon which Reilly and McIntire's description of PSE rests bear any resemblance to the language produced in a natural language contact situation. The data collected by Myles-Zitzer (1990) (see description of the study in Chapter 1) are somewhat more reliable in that the researcher controlled for the variable of language learning background: The same narrative was produced by a native Deaf signer to three subjects, two hearing second-language learners of ASL demonstrating varying degrees of proficiency and a first-generation Deaf signer of ASL. However, it is clear that a narrative is a less spontaneous linguistic event than a conversation, particularly if it is produced three times. Furthermore, the sample in this study is relatively small.

Another problem with earlier studies of language contact in the American deaf community concerns the extent of knowledge about the structure of ASL itself at the time that the studies were done. In general, sociolinguistic descriptions tend to follow (or at least to accompany but, generally, not to precede) linguistic descriptions of a language or a variety, and it is only recently that a fundamental empirical understanding of ASL structure has become available. Indeed, there are many aspects of ASL structure that are still being debated, while other aspects await even the most basic descriptive attention. Accordingly, the sociolinguistic interaction between ASL and other kinds of signing cannot be described or understood without a basic understanding of the linguistic systems in question. For example, we cannot describe and understand code switching between ASL and other kinds of signing unless we have a clear picture of what is part of the ASL system and what is not. It does not seem, for example, that some rules in ASL, such as negative incorporation or agent–beneficiary directionality, identified in earlier studies as variable, are indeed variable (Woodward, 1973a). But we suggest that such identification came about in part due to what was known about the structure of ASL at the time of the study. We hope that our description of language contact in the American deaf community reflects the most recent descriptions of ASL structure.

It is clear that any study that proposes to describe the linguistic outcome of language contact in the American deaf community should at the very least use data collected in naturalistic interactional settings that reflect actual language contact situations as closely as possible. That is precisely what we attempted to do in the design and implementation of our data collection. In Chapter 1, we listed possible language contact situations that might occur in the American deaf community, according to participant characteristics. Since one of our original goals was to reexamine claims that had been made about linguistic outcomes, specifically that PSE was the result of deaf–hearing interaction, the focus of our data collection was on the first situation listed: the interaction of Deaf bilinguals with hearing bilinguals. In short, we wanted to make sure that we were controlling as much as possible for signing skills and that what we were eliciting was the result of language contact and not a function of second-language learning. We wanted to be sure that all of the participants were skilled ASL users. We also wanted to take a step in the direction of making the data more representative of the American deaf community by including black signers among the informants and judges. Clearly, future studies of language contact will need to include Asian, Hispanic, and native American signers. This observation is not simply an abstract reflection of current concerns with multiculturalism. Rather, there is emerging evidence of the unique linguistic reality of bicultural deaf individuals in the United States. For example, research is being done on deaf Navajos in Arizona who know ASL as a result of attendance at residential schools for the deaf, as well as their indigenous sign language, about which little is known as yet (Davis and Supalla, 1991).

Our informants included six dyads of white signers and four dyads and two triads of black signers. The composition of all of the dyads and triads is summarized in Tables 5 and 6. (One way of recruiting informants was to ask one informant to come to the interview and to bring a friend. The two triads are explained by the simple fact that three people showed up for the interviews instead of two, and we saw no reason to exclude the third person.) Eleven of the twelve white informants rated themselves as very skilled in ASL, and all twelve rated themselves as skilled in English. Nine of the twelve were born deaf, one was born hard of hearing and is now deaf, and two were born hearing and became deaf at 15 months of age and 3 years of age, respectively. Five of the twelve white informants came from deaf families, and of the remaining seven, five attended residential schools for the deaf and learned ASL at an early age. One white informant learned ASL from other deaf students in a mainstream program. One white informant learned ASL at age 21.

TABLE 5
Composition of White Dyads

Dyad	Participant A	Participant B
1	Deaf family, born deaf, residential school	Deaf family, deaf at 15 mos., public school
2	Deaf family, born deaf, deaf day school	Deaf family, born hard of hearing, now profoundly deaf, deaf day school
3	Deaf family, born deaf, residential school	Hearing family, born deaf, residential school
4	Hearing family, born deaf, residential school	Hearing family, deaf at age 3, residential school
5	Hearing family, born deaf, residential school	Hearing family, born deaf, mainstream program
6	Hearing family, deaf at age 3, residential school	Hearing family, born deaf, learned ASL at age 21, public school

TABLE 6
Composition of Black Dyads and Triads

	Participant A	Participant B	Participant C
Dyad 7	Deaf at age 3, hearing family, mainstreamed, then residential school at age 9	Born deaf, hearing family, residential school	
Dyad 8	Born deaf, hearing family, main-streamed, then residential school at age 11	Born deaf, hearing family, main-streamed, then MSSD[a] at age 13	
Dyad 9	Born deaf, hearing family, residential school	Deaf at 7 months, hearing family, mainstreamed, then residential school at age 10	
Dyad 10	Born deaf, hearing family, main-streamed, resi-dential school at age 10	Hard of hearing, became deaf at age 15, main- streamed, then residential school at age 12	
Triad 11	Early onset, hearing family (deaf sister), then KDES at age 11	Born deaf, hearing family, residential school	Born hearing, deaf at age 8½, deaf family, main-streamed, then residential school at age 15
Triad 12	Born deaf, hearing family, residential school at age 4	Born deaf, hearing family KDES at age 6	Born deaf, hearing family, KDES at age 3

[a]MSSD: Model Secondary School for the Deaf; KDES: Kendall Demonstration Elementary School, both located on Kendall Green with Gallaudet University.

As concerns the black informants, we draw a distinction between the informants in dyads 7, 8, 9, and 10, and the two triads. In dyads 7, 8, 9, and 10, all informants are from hearing families, and only two are early learners of ASL, having entered residential schools as small children. (In fact, informant 9A has hearing parents who worked in a residential school and signed.) The other six informants in these dyads were all mainstreamed and did not enter residential schools until late childhood or early adolescence, making them relatively late learners of ASL. One of the informants in the triads is from a Deaf family and the remaining five informants in the triads are all early learners of ASL.

During the data collection, video cameras were present, but at no point were the technicians visible. The sign production of the dyads and triads was videotaped during interaction with, first, a Deaf interviewer who signed ASL; then the dyad alone; next with a hearing interviewer, a nonnative signer who introduced herself as hearing; then the dyad or triad alone again; finally with the Deaf interviewer again. The whole interview experience began with exclusive contact with the Deaf interviewer. The white informants participated in one interview that included the five different situations outlined above. As there is some research evidence that black signers' signing varies as a function of ethnicity of the interlocutor, the black informants participated in two interviews, one with black interviewers and one with white interviewers.[6] The structure of the interviews with black informants is summarized in Table 7.

The interview with the white informants and the first interview with the black informants consisted of a discussion of several broad topics of interest to members of the deaf community. Four statements were presented and participants were asked if they agreed or disagreed, and why. In the second interview, black dyad participants were presented with three other statements and asked to agree or disagree; black triad informants were presented four statements.[7]

6. A goal for future research is to conduct similar interviews with white informants and black interviewers, to have comparable data for all informants.

7. Interview questions asked of informants are as follows.
First interview (all informants)
1. Suppose you are in a public place, like an airport or a restaurant, and someone finds out that you are deaf and wants to help you. That's OK. Agree or disagree?
2. The hearing children of deaf parents are members of deaf culture. Agree or disagree?
3. Residential schools are better than mainstreaming. Agree or disagree?
4. Gallaudet University should have a deaf president. Agree or disagree?
Second interview (black informants)
1. Remember Jane Bassett Spillman's remark that "Deaf people are not ready to function in the hearing world . . ." Agree or disagree?
2. Black deaf people have the same educational opportunities as white deaf people. Agree or disagree?
3. Most black deaf people say that they are black first and deaf second. Agree or disagree?
(black triads)
4. What do you think of the current communication controversy on campus?

TABLE 7
Structure of the Interviews with Black Informants

Situation	First interview	Second interview
(1) With deaf interviewer (interruption)	White interviewer	Black interviewer
(2) Informants left alone		
(3) With hearing interviewer (interruption)	White interviewer	Black interviewer
(4) Informants left alone		
(5) With deaf interviewer	White interviewer	Black interviewer

The interview structure has parallels with Edwards' (1986) research design for a study of British black English. The major concern in that study was the improvement of methodology "so as to ensure that this corpus authentically reflects the range of individual and situational variation which exists within the black community" (p. 9). Edwards (1986) recognized the obvious need for the black interviewers to gain access to vernacular speech and was assured that the presence of a sympathetic, young black interviewer, that is, a peer, would guarantee the use of the vernacular by the informants. But

> Our observation made it clear that many young black people use Patois only in in-group conversation, so that the presence of any other person, even the young black fieldworker, would be enough to inhibit Patois usage. The obvious solution was to create a situation in which the young people were left alone. [p. 17]

Our study also reflects the same concerns as a study reported by Rickford and McNair-Knox (1991) which focuses on addressee- and topic-influenced style shift. As in the Edwards study, the informants in our study were left alone twice during each interview and asked to continue discussing the topics introduced by the interviewers. In the first instance, the Deaf interviewer was called away for "an emergency phone call." After 8 to 10 minutes, the hearing interviewer arrived and explained that she would be taking the Deaf interviewer's place. The interview continued and the hearing interviewer then left to check on the Deaf interviewer. The dyad or triad was again left alone until the return of the Deaf interviewer, and the Deaf interviewer then completed the interview. Following the completion of the interview, the informants were told that there had in fact been no emergency, and the reason for the Deaf interviewer's departure was explained. The informants all viewed portions of the tapes and the purpose of the study was explained to them. They were all given the option to have their tapes erased on the spot, if they felt that they did not want their interview to be included in the data. No one exercised this option. They were all glad to be told that the "emergency" was false, but accepted it as part of the data-collection procedure.

Each interview lasted between 30 and 40 minutes, the result being a substantial corpus of language use. The total number of informants was 26.

The Big Picture

We can now describe the overall pattern of language use during the interviews. The distributional pattern of language use with the white informants is summarized in Fig. 4. On the left-hand side of each pattern, we see the five situations in which the informants found themselves. Across the top, we see abbreviations for the language used: American Sign Language (ASL), contact signing (CS), and Signed English (SE). In cases where there was rapid switching between ASL and contact signing, we described the language use as ASL/CS. In other cases, there was switching between contact signing and Signed English, which we designated CS/SE. 1A refers to one informant in the first dyad, 1B to the second informant in that dyad, and so forth. The judgments of overall language use during the interviews were made by the researchers. ASL and contact signing (other than ASL) were identified by a deaf native signer; Signed English consistently included the use of voice and hence included input from the hearing researcher. These judgments preceded the judgment of specific clips from the tapes by a total of 30 judges, which we will describe in another part of this chapter. The description of the linguistic features of contact signing is based on the latter. We can see three distinct patterns of language

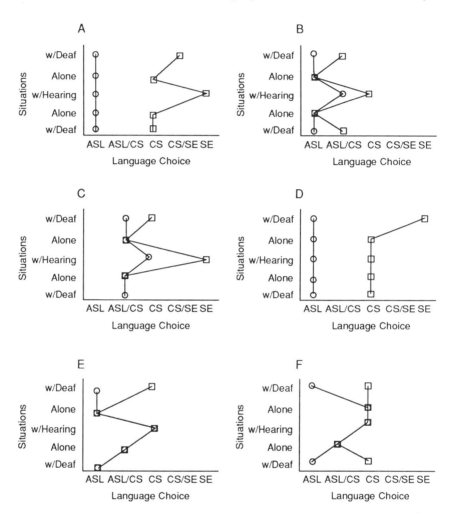

Figure 4   Patterns of language choice with white informants; (A) dyad 1; (B) dyad 2; (C) dyad 3; (D) dyad 4; (E) dyad 5; (F) dyad 6. (Lucas and Valli 1989, p. 25. In C. Lucas (Ed.) *The Sociolinguistics of the Deaf Community.* Academic Press.

use in Fig. 4. One pattern, as seen with dyads 1 and 4, consists of the two informants using distinctly different kinds of signing and never overlapping with each other. For example, in dyad 1, informant 1A consistently uses ASL throughout the interview, even though 1B starts out with contact signing and Signed English, then moves first to contact signing, then to Signed English, and then back to contact signing. Similarly, in dyad 4, informant 4A consistently uses ASL, while 4B starts out with Signed English and then consistently uses contact signing. Neither 1B nor 4B ever approaches the use of ASL during the interview. The first pattern, then, is that one participant's choice of signing during the interview is consistently distinct from the coparticipant's choice or choices.

In dyads 2 and 6, we see a second pattern, where the informants use different kinds of signing during the first part of the interview with the deaf interviewer but, when left alone with each other, use the same kind of signing. In dyad 2, informant 2A continues with ASL, and 2B switches to ASL; in dyad 6, informant 6B continues with contact signing, and 6A switches to contact signing. In dyad 6, the informants use the same kind of signing and switch in the same way toward ASL when left alone and sign quite differently with the deaf interviewer. In dyad 2, the informants do not sign in exactly the same way, but they do shift in the same direction. Also noteworthy in both dyads is the fact that, despite shifting during the interview, each informant signs the same way with the deaf interviewer at the end of the interview as at the beginning.

The third pattern is seen in dyads 3 and 5, where the informants begin the interview with different kinds of signing. One informant then shifts toward the other, and then both informants either use the same kind of signing for the remainder of the interview (dyad 5) or use the same kind of signing, then shift in the same direction, and together use the same kind of signing again (dyad 3).

Figures 5 and 6 show the overall patterns of language use for the black informants. As with the white informants, the black participants used language differently in different situations. For example, in dyad 7, participant 7A begins with contact signing in the presence of the black Deaf interviewer, signs more ASL when the dyad is left alone, moves back to contact signing when the white hearing interviewer appears, and continues with contact signing until the black Deaf interviewer reappears, at which point 7A uses ASL. This in contrast to 7B who, while *describing* herself as a skilled ASL user and *demonstrating* ASL skill in informal settings, never uses ASL during the interview and alternates between contact signing and contact signing with voice, the latter a distinction that appeared with the black informants (CS/v). As we remarked earlier, black signers and white signers make different language choices depend-

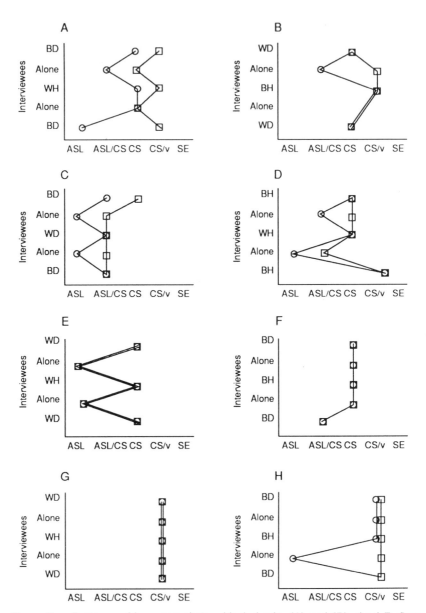

Figure 5   Patterns of language choice, black dyads; (A) and (B), dyad 7, first and second interview; (C) and (D), dyad 8, first and second interview; (E) and (F), dyad 9, first and second interview; (G) and (H), dyad 10, first and second interview. BD, black deaf interviewer; WH, white hearing interviewer; BH, black hearing interviewer, WD, white deaf interviewer.

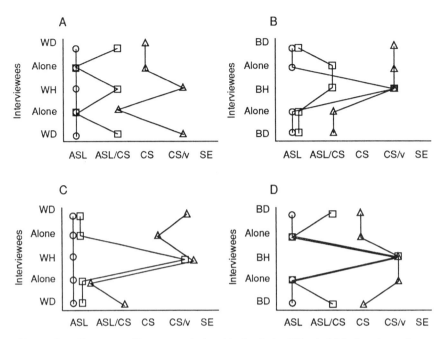

Figure 6   Patterns of language choice, black triads; (A) triad 11, first interview;
(B) triad 11, second interview; (C) triad 12, first interview; (D) triad 12, second
interview. WD, white deaf interviewer; WH, white hearing interviewer; BD, black
deaf interviewer; BH, black hearing interviewer.

ing on the situation. However, we notice some differences in the
overall patterns. For example, the black signers never display the
first pattern described for the white signers, that is, two people
doing two different things with no overlap. There is always some
overlap in signers' behavior with the black informants. We do see
the second pattern, in which signers start out differently and then
converge, as in dyads 11 and 12, and we see a pattern similar to the
third, in which signers shift in the same direction, as with informants 11A and 11C. We also see a fourth pattern with the black
informants which we saw only with a portion of one white dyad (5),
that is, informants doing exactly the same thing all the way through
the interview. We see this with both interviews conducted with
dyad 9 and with one interview with dyad 10. As with the white
informants, some black informants—7B, 10A, and 10B—never use
ASL. Some only use ASL: 11B and 12A. We also find differences
between dyads 7, 8, 9, and 10 and triads 11 and 12. In 7, 8, 9, and

10, the informants use some ASL with the black deaf and the white deaf interviewers, but none at all with the hearing interviewers, black or white. They also use no Signed English. With the hearing interviewers, they use contact signing, regardless of the race of the interviewer. The signers in the two triads show less convergence than informants in 7, 8, 9, and 10, and they are more like the white informants in that, in one interview situation, three participants may be using two or three different modes simultaneously. For example, in triad 11, the interview begins with the white deaf interviewer using ASL. Informant 11B uses ASL; 11A uses ASL with some contact signing, but 11C begins with contact signing and does not use ASL until the group is left alone for the second time. The triad informants also use a lot more ASL than the dyad participants. Given this description of overall language use during the interviews, we will now provide some accounting of what we found.

Accounting for the Patterns of
Language Use

Before providing some account of the overall patterns of language use during the interviews, we should briefly talk about what we had predicted and what we hadn't predicted. It will be recalled that our initial focus had been on the interaction between deaf and hearing signers, as one of our original goals had been to reexamine claims about the linguistic outcomes of that interaction. In light of our findings, it seems very ironic that in designing the structure of the interviews, the situations with the deaf interviewers and the situations in which the informants were left alone were originally included as *controls.* That is, because of the "received knowledge" about language contact in the deaf community, we had simply assumed that Deaf native ASL signers would produce ASL with other Deaf native ASL signers, being either the Deaf interviewer or the other informant. Our original focus was on the shift to contact signing that we had predicted in the presence of the hearing interviewers. And we did find Deaf people using ASL with each other and contact signing with the hearing interviewers, as predicted. However, what we also found—and had not predicted—was (1) Deaf ASL native users using contact signing with each other with no hearing people present, (2) ASL being used with the hearing interviewers, and (3) situations in which as many as three individuals used three different modes simultaneously. The observations on the overall pattern of language use during the interviews can be summarized as follows:

- Some informants use contact signing or Signed English with the hearing interviewer, as expected; others use ASL throughout.
- ASL is used with the hearing interviewer by some informants but not others.
- Contact signing is produced with the deaf interviewer and when informants are alone.
- ASL is used not only by deaf informants from Deaf families but also by deaf informants from hearing families.

These observations appear to challenge the traditional perspective on language contact in the American deaf community. For example, it has been traditionally assumed that contact signing (known as PSE) appears in deaf–hearing interaction, mainly for the obvious reason that the hearing person might not understand ASL. On the extreme is the position that the very purpose of contact signing is to prevent hearing people from learning ASL (Woodward and Markowicz, 1975). More measured approaches simply describe contact signing as the product of deaf–hearing interaction. Little is said, however, about the use of contact signing in exclusively deaf settings. Although the need for comprehension might explain the occurrence of contact signing in deaf–hearing interaction, it is clearly not an issue in portions of the interviews in which all of the participants are native or near-native signers and, in some instances, sign ASL with each other. The choice to use contact signing with other Deaf ASL natives, then, appears to be motivated by sociolinguistic factors. Two such factors are the relative formality of the interview situation (including the inevitable presence of videotape equipment) and the participant's lack of familiarity in some cases with both the interviewer and the other informant. The data also clearly present counterevidence to the claim that deaf people never or rarely sign ASL in the presence of hearing people, as four informants chose to sign ASL throughout their respective interviews. This choice may be motivated by a third sociolinguistic factor, that is, the desire to establish one's identity as a bona fide member of the Deaf community or cultural group, a desire that may supersede considerations of formality and lack of familiarity with one's cointerlocutor(s). Clearly, different sociolinguistic factors motivate the language choices of different individuals. We do see switching motivated by the presence of the hearing interviewer, but we also see other factors at work. Factors such as the formality of the situation and the lack of familiarity of the informants with the deaf interviewer and with each other reveal attitudes about the kind of signing that is appropriate in different situations. Indeed, it is this interrelationship between language attitudes and language choices that prompted Stokoe (1969) to describe the language situation in the deaf community as diglossic—that is, ASL strictly in some contexts and a more English-like signing strictly for other contexts, with no overlap. We recall here the history of language use in deaf education, in which, after 1880, the use of English was required and the use of ASL was restricted or banned outright, and we see this history as the probable origin of these patterns of language use. We suggest that deaf individuals learn at a very early age that ASL is not appropriate in classroom situations. Since interaction in classroom situations has been for the most part with hearing teachers and since, other than parents and relatives, teachers are the main early contact with the hearing world, the extension of the argument is that ASL is not appropriate with hearing people at all, and if one is using ASL upon the approach of a hearing person, it is appropriate to switch to a more English-like signing. Finally, since classroom situations are relatively formal, the non-use of ASL extends to other relatively formal situations, such as videotaped interviews. There is also another common attitude, documented by Kannapell (1985; 1989) that the use of more English-like signing shows that the signer is well educated and smart, while the use of ASL shows that the signer is not educated and dumb. In a situation in which an informant is not familiar with the other informants, it is possible that that attitude may also be at work. However, as we pointed out earlier, while the characterization of the language situation in the deaf community as diglossic has been widely accepted by laymen and professionals alike, it has been challenged by some researchers, for example Lee (1982), whose work we discussed in Chapter 1. And we suggest that our data also call into question a characterization of the situation as diglossic. Clearly, some informants see ASL as inappropriate for any part of the interview. However, some informants see ASL as appropriate when no interviewer is present, and some informants use ASL in all of the situations, with no apparent regard for formality, familiarity, or audiological status of the interlocutor(s).

There is a fourth factor which may play a role in language choices during the interviews, and that concerns the age at which an informant acquired ASL. It will be recalled that we make a distinction between the four black dyads (7, 8, 9, and 10) and the two black triads (11 and 12). Six of the eight informants in dyads 7, 8, 9, and 10 learned ASL as adolescents, as opposed to the informants in the triads, all but one of whom are native or early learners of ASL. The behavior of the informants in the triads parallels the behavior of the white informants, all of whom are native or early learners, and we suggest that age of acquisition may play some role in sociolinguistic choices later on. In general, native or early learners used more ASL with hearing people and were involved in more situations in which more than one made was used simultaneously.

The overall patterns of language use during the interviews provide an illustration of Giles' (1977) theory of accommodation in linguistic behavior (also see Valli, 1988). Accommodation can take the form of convergence, nonconvergence, or divergence. With convergence, a speaker chooses a language variety that seems to fit the needs of the cointerlocutor(s). Under some conditions, however, a speaker can diverge in order to dissociate from the cointerlocutors, perhaps to emphasize loyalty to his group. Nonconvergence occurs when one speaker does not move away from another but simply continues using a variety that differs from other speakers. In the case of the white informants in our data, all of the B informants except 6B converged toward the A informants, which is to say toward ASL. We suggest that in dyad 6, participant A may converge toward B because B learned ASL relatively late (at age 21) and may not feel comfortable using ASL. The convergence–divergence–nonconvergence situation with the black informants is not as straightforward. We see ASL users converging toward contact signing, contact signing users converging toward ASL and, in general, a lot more idiosyncratic behavior, particularly among the early or native learners. As we mentioned earlier, we see complete convergence in dyad 9 and in dyad 10's first interview.

Finally, the overall patterns of language use reveal situations in which three different participants (this may include the interviewer) are using three different modes simultaneously. This is a phenomenon of bilingualism that has been seen in spoken language situations. For example, Gal (1979) describes situations in which one person speaks Hungarian while another speaks German, in her study of language use in Oberwart, Austria. Chipewya and Cree are used by different interlocutors in a study done by Scollon and Scollon (1979), while a husband and a wife speak genetically unrelated languages to each other in the Solomon Islands, as reported by Lincoln (1979). Salisbury (1962) reports a trilingual conversation in New Guinea. So it would appear that the bilinguals in our study are not unique, that they behave like the bilinguals in spoken language situations. It is interesting to note that in the cases in our data, there is never any overt comment about the simultaneous use of two or three different modes. Presumably, the informants have made an assessment of the situation and feel entirely comfortable using a mode that differs from the mode used by a cointerlocutor, understand what is being signed to them, and assume that they are being understood.

This concludes our discussion of the overall patterns of language use observed during the interviews. We will now describe the judgment process by which the videotaped segments were selected which form the data base for our linguistic description of contact signing.

When Is ASL? The Issue of Judgments

As we have explained, one of the original goals of our project was to provide a description of the linguistic features of contact signing. The first step in achieving that goal was to elicit naturalistic examples of contact signing. The second step was to create a data base of a reasonable size for analysis. We did not feel that judgments as to which portions of the videotaped interviews were ASL and which portions were contact signing should be limited to the researchers. We felt that it was imperative to have a justifiable number of native signer judges providing judgments about the language used on the videotapes. Then, given agreement on the contact signing portions of the tapes, we could proceed with our description of its linguistic features. In this section, we will describe the process and the results of the judging process.

Numerous spoken language researchers have used judgments of language use as a central component of their studies. Language attitudes studies (for example, Bouchard-Ryan, 1973; Hoover, 1978; Light, Richard, and Bell, 1978; Rosenthal, 1974) have investigated users' attitudes toward languages or varieties of language by requiring them to respond to audiotapes or fill out questionnaires. Other studies (for example, Anisfeld and Lambert, 1963; Lambert *et al.*, 1960; Shuy, Baratz, and Wolfram, 1969; Williams, 1970; Williams, Whitehead, and Miller, 1971; Williams, Whitehead, and Traupmann, 1971) have required native users to judge the demographic or personality characteristics of speakers whose language usage was recorded on audiotape. Finally, other studies similar to ours have required native users to rate the relative fluency and accentedness of tape-recorded speakers, in attempts to isolate the specific linguistic variables that shape judgments (see, for example, Graff, Labov, and Harris, 1986; Brennan, Brennan, and Dawson, 1975; Chiasson-Lavoie and Laberge, 1971; Grebler, More, and Guzman, 1970; Muench, 1971; Palmer, 1973; Thompson, 1975; and Williams *et al.*, 1971).

Our study has in common with the latter group of studies the fact that it requires raters to focus strictly on linguistic events, as opposed to providing attitudinal evaluations based on linguistic events. In all other studies, however, the basic structural nature of the linguistic events being judged was not at issue. The focus may have been on the relative accentedness or fluency of a code, but the very status of the code as English or Spanish or French was not at issue. In our study, the structural nature of the contact signing *is* the central issue, and the native signers' judgments play a key role in defining and describing its features. This is similar to a study by Chana and Romaine (1984) in which Panjabi/English bilinguals were asked to judge not different language or varieties/accents of the same language, but varieties which draw on two languages, Panjabi and English. Ten judges listened to eight samples produced by one speaker, the samples showing varying degrees of code switching. The judges were asked to evaluate the characteristics of the speech and the person speaking. Results showed that the same speaker was evaluated different ways, depending on how he spoke, and that different types of code-switched discourse were related to external dimensions, such as perceived fluency in English and Panjabi, intelligibility, and expressivity. For example, there was consensus among the judges about the relation between the type of code-switched discourse produced and the perceived fluency of the speaker in Panjabi or English.

As we described earlier, the interviews included 26 people in 18 separate interviews (1 interview each for each white dyad, 2 interviews each for each black dyad and triad). Each interview averaged 40 minutes in length, the result being approximately 12 hours of videotape. Our original plan for the judgment process had been to have native signers view the interviews in their entirety and to indicate by means of pressing a button points at which shifts away from and back to ASL took place. We did hire four native signers to do this and, though they completed the task, it became obvious that it was too time consuming. We wanted to have enough judges to have reliable judgments, and it was not practical to have the number of judges required view all of the tapes. The solution was to select representative 30-second clips from the videotapes, clips that had been judged by the researchers and the four "master judges" to be either clearly ASL or "not ASL." These master judges were native ASL signers who were either teaching ASL or involved in ASL research and demonstrated a facility with the metalinguistics of ASL. That is, they could easily explain their judgments in linguistic terms. And the labeling of clips was also based, of course, on our own knowledge and understanding of what is and what is not ASL structure. The number of clips was determined by what we thought we could reasonably expect from the judges in terms of time commitment and attention span. A total of 20 clips was selected, representative of all of the informants and all of the interview situations (i.e., with the deaf interviewer, alone, and with the hearing interviewer). Five of the clips were judged by the master judges to be clearly ASL, and 15 were judged to be "not ASL." The clips were presented twice to each judge, each time in a different random order. That is, each judge saw 20 randomly ordered clips and then saw the same clips in a different random order. All of the clips were edited onto one tape and there was a short break between the two presentations. Upon seeing each clip, each judge was asked to simply write down whether that clip was ASL or "not ASL." The entire task took about 30 minutes.

The judgment task was completed by a total of 30 judges. The sample size determination for comparing two binomial proportions demanding a 5% error rate was determined using standard formulae. The calculation of the sample size was based on two a priori assumptions: (1) Given the characteristics of the judges we had selected (i.e., Deaf ASL users who had learned ASL natively or at a very early age), presented with an ASL clip they would judge it as such 80% of the time; and (2) the same judges had a 50% chance of judging a "not" clip as "not ASL." Based on these assumptions, the sample size was determined to be 24. That is, 24 people would have to view each clip to ensure no more than a 5% error rate, of two types. A Type 1 error rate would concern a clip that was truly ASL judged to be "not ASL"; a Type 2 error rate would concern a "not ASL" clip judged to be ASL. We decided to round the number of judges up to 30.

Having determined the number of judges required, we implemented the judgment task. As the task proceeded, we naturally analyzed and compared the judgments and an interesting pattern began to emerge which led us to divide the judges into three groups as opposed to two and to recruit judges with particular characteristics. We had originally intended for all of the judges to be members of the Deaf community at large, and specifically not sign language teachers or linguists. However, we began to notice a significant difference between the judgments made by people who had studied ASL structure and had an awareness of its status as a language and the judgments of people who did not demonstrate such exposure or awareness. We decided early on to control for these factors in the judging process, such that the final pool of judges included 11 "naive" white judges, 8 "naive" black judges, and 11 linguists and ASL teachers (1 black, the rest white). By "significant difference," we mean that the judgments of the linguists and teachers tended to agree with the judgments of the master judges, while those of the "naive" judges tended to be different.

Our original plan was to select from the 15 "not ASL" clips those clips for which there was at least 85% agreement among all of the judges and to base our description of contact signing on those. We had predicted that there would be at least 10 such clips. However, what we predicted was quite different from what actually happened during the judgment task.

Table 8 presents the overall results of the judgment task. (The raw percentages appear in Appendix I.) The table should be read as follows. The numbers across the top represent the number of the clip. It should be remembered that this represents the first order and that the clips occurred in a different order for the second viewing. Under the clip numbers are the master judgments and the race of the informant being judged, B or W. The letters D, H, and A indicate whether the informant being judged was in a situation with the deaf interviewer, the hearing interviewer, or alone with the other informant. The clips themselves were edited so that a judge only saw one person and not the other informant(s). The percentages shown represent the average of the first and second judgments of a given segment by the judges in each of the three groups. For example, all of the linguists (100%) judged clip #1 to be ASL, in agreement with the master judges. Likewise the "naive" white judges, while 81% of the "naive" black judges judged the same clip to be ASL. For clip #15, which the master judges judged to be "not ASL," 90% of the linguists and teachers agreed, while only 63% of the "naive" white judges and 18% of the "naive" black judges judged this clip as "not ASL." Since the judges were given two choices, this means that 37% of the "naive" white judges and 82% of the "naive" black judges judged this clip to be ASL! We will return to why that might happen later in our discussion. At this point, the overall results of the judging process deserve some attention. For instance, only with clip #18, an ASL clip, is there complete agreement among the three groups, and even with that clip, 19% still judged it to be "not ASL." For the other 19 clips, there is no one pattern of judgment. There is some agreement between two groups, but never between all three. There are cases in which the judgment of the linguists and teachers differs radically from both the black and the white community members, as in clip #7; there

TABLE 8

Percentage of Agreement with Master Judgments[a]

Clip #	1	2	3	4	5	6	7	8	9	10	11	12	13	14	15	16	17	18	19	20
Master judgment	ASL	NA	NA	NA	NA	NA	NA	NA	NA	ASL	NA	ASL	NA	NA	NA	NA	ASL	ASL	NA	NA
	W[b]	W	W	B	W	B	W	W	W	B	B	W	B	B	W	B	W	B	W	B
	D	H	D	D	H	D	A	H	H	A	A	A	A	D	H	A	H	D	D	A
Linguists	100	100	81	39	50	95	81	81	100	90	59	86	63	100	90	18	100	81	100	81
White community	100	100	100	13	36	90	36	63	95	90	36	81	63	63	63	9	95	81	72	81
Black community	81	75	50	50	31	62	43	75	68	87	43	56	37	18	43	0	75	81	37	18
All	95	91	80	30	40	85	55	73	88	90	46	76	56	65	68	10	88	81	73	65

[a]Percentages are average of first and second judgments.
[b]W, white informant; B, black informant; D, with deaf interviewer; H, with hearing interviewer; A, informants alone; NA, not ASL.

are cases in which the linguists and teachers and white community members differ from the black community members, as in clips #20 and 13; and there are cases of complete disagreement among all three groups, as in clips #4, 5, 14, 15, 16, and 19. In the next section, we will examine the linguistic features of each clip (and a transcript of each clip is provided in Appendix II) and try to account for the source of the disagreement among the judges. At this point, the disagreement seems to have two implications, one specific and one general.

The specific implication concerns our project and the analysis of contact signing. We had predicted that we would end up with at least 10 clips which judges would agree were "not ASL" upon which we could base our description. However, were we to arbitrarily pick, say, an 85% agreement rate as an acceptable rate to choose a clip for description, only 3 clips would qualify. Indeed, some of the highest percentages of agreement occur with the ASL clips: 95% for #1, 90% for #10, 76% for #12, 88% for #17, and 81% for #18. Since the variables of exposure to and awareness of ASL structure seemed to play a significant role in rate of agreement with the master judgments, we decided, for the purposes of analysis, to group together the clips for which the linguists and teachers showed 80% or more agreement with the master judgments. There are 10 "not ASL" clips which fit this description: clips #2, 3, 6, 7, 8, 9, 14, 15, 19, and 20. We will examine 9 of these clips as contact signing clips and provide a description of their features. Clip #9, in which the informant is audibly speaking English and signing, is best described as an example of Sign Supported Speech. We will also look at the 5 clips (#4, 5, 11, 13, and 16) for which there was complete disagreement with the master judgments and among the groups, to try to determine what might account for the disagreement.

The general implication of the disagreement in judgments has to do with the status of language in the Deaf community in 1991. As we pointed out, we were very careful in the selection of the judges to make sure that they were indeed either native ASL users or very early learners, and we feel that we controlled carefully for the variable of "judge receptive ASL competence," that is, we felt confident that our judges would know ASL when they saw it and would easily distinguish it from "not ASL." And it will be recalled that our rationale for selecting 30 judges hinged on an a priori assumption that competent ASL signers would indeed know ASL when they saw it. In fact, part of our confidence came from a pilot judgment task that we did at the conference on Theoretical Issues in Sign Language Research in Boston in May, 1990. We selected five judges at random from the audience, all native Deaf signers, and asked them to judge 4 clips, 2 ASL and 2 "not ASL." And the result was 100% agreement with the master judgments. We then came back to Washington and implemented our judgment task, with the results reported here. What we had overlooked in Boston, of course, was that all 5 of the pilot judges fit the category we had yet to define, "linguists and language teachers," people with a fairly sophisticated metalinguistic knowledge of ASL. Looking back, we realized that the context of a theoretical sign language linguistics conference is a very special one and that we should not be surprised by our results. The general observation is that, at this point, one can by no means assume that just because someone is a competent user of ASL he or she can look at signing production and reliably say "That's ASL" or "That's not ASL." We cannot just take a group of Deaf ASL users "off the street" and predict agreement in judgment. It would appear that our a priori assumptions were just wrong. The most reliable judgments come from people who have metalinguistic knowledge of ASL, because they are linguists or sign language teachers or have been exposed to ASL linguistics through workshops or courses. We suggest that the situation is as it is because of the history of deaf education and specifically because of the role of ASL in that history. We will recall that for most of the history of deaf education, the use of ASL was forbidden or, at best, tolerated, and even in the early years when it was accepted its linguistic structure was certainly not being described or analyzed. Such description and analysis did not begin until the early 1960s with Stokoe. One conclusion that the outcome of our judgment task suggests is that many adult ASL users, while completely competent and skilled in the use of the language, have a hard time differentiating between ASL and contact signing that, while it may incorporate many ASL features, also incorporates many English features or even idiosyncratic ones and cannot be said to be ASL from a linguistic standpoint. This is why we have entitled this section *"When* is ASL?,"* as opposed to *"What* is ASL,"* because it appears that a judgment as to the occurrence of ASL has at least something to do with the judge's metalinguistic knowledge. But it is also very important to understand and to keep in perspective the nature of metalinguistic knowledge itself: that is, the very activities of doing linguistic research, making dictionaries, and devising curricula for the teaching of a language ultimately have the effect of determining what is part of the language and what is not; these activities have the effect of shaping metalinguistic knowledge. The makers of dictionaries and curricula necessarily make judgments about what is part of the language and what is not, and often those judgments shape the notion of what the language is. Of course, those judgments may often be contradicted by everyday use of the language. Furthermore, very often activities such as the making of dictionaries of a language often have the purpose not only of describing the structure of the language but of establishing the status of a linguistic system as "a language." That is, dictionary making and other linguistic activities are also social and political activities. Our point here is that while it is true that the judges with more metalinguistic knowledge provided the most "reliable" judgments, it is hard, if not impossible, to establish objective criteria for saying what is and is not part of a linguistic system, and that metalinguistic knowledge itself may be shaped by factors other than purely linguistic ones. The fact that the "linguist" judges were reliable merely means that their judgments were in line with current knowledge about the structure of ASL, knowledge which necessarily reflects sociolinguistic reality as well as linguistic reality. Further evidence of this came from a small pilot study that we did as part of the project. Three videotaped clips of the same signer (one ASL clip and two contact signing clips) were shown to two sets of judges. One set of judges came from Deaf families and were native ASL signers; the other set came from hearing families and had learned ASL later. In addition, one set of judges was told that the signer they were seeing came from a Deaf family and was a native signer, while the other set of judges was told that the same person came from a hearing family and had learned ASL later. The results of the pilot study indicated that what the judges were told about the signer influenced their judgment of the kind of signing being produced (Lucas and Valli, 1991). There are parallels with minority spoken language situations, in which competent speakers of the minority language judge that language to be something else. For example, S. Romaine (personal communication) reports that in the early days of Tok Pisin use, its speakers sometimes thought that it was English, while now most people are aware that Tok Pisin and English are different.

The Linguistic Features of Contact Signing

As we explained in the previous section, our description of the linguistic features of contact signing is based upon the nine clips for which the linguist and teacher judges showed 80% or better agreement with the master judgments. And as we mentioned earlier, one of the unexpected findings of the project was the use of contact signing by Deaf people with no hearing people present. As it happens, of the nine clips we will describe, three are from portions of the interview with the hearing interviewer, four are with the Deaf interviewer, and two are from when the informants were alone, that is, with another Deaf person. So six of the nine clips show contact signing among Deaf people.

Table 9 summarizes the features of contact signing which we have isolated in all of the clips. Readers familiar with our preliminary description of the features of contact signing (Lucas and Valli, 1989) will notice additions to the inventory of features. The earlier description was indeed preliminary, these additions being the natural consequence of an analysis based on a much larger data base.

Lexical Forms

Most of the lexical forms found in contact signing are ASL signs and ASL-like signs. By the latter, we mean signs that are constructed in the same way that ASL signs are, that is, composed of movement and hold segments, with handshape, location, orientation, and nonmanual signals, but that are not used in ASL. A good example of an ASL-like sign is the sign BECAUSE. We could say that it is composed of a sequence of a hold, a movement, and a hold, that it begins with an L handshape that changes to an X handshape, and that it is produced at the forehead location with the palm

Table 9

Linguistic Features of Contact Signing (Based on 14 Clips)

Lexical form	Lexical meaning and function	Morphological structure	Syntactic structure
ASL and ASL-like lexical items, English mouthing, single isolated spoken English words, English whispering	ASL, English, idiosyncratic	Reduced ASL and English; some inflected ASL verbs; some signs for English inflections (#ING, #MENT), ASL nonmanuals	Reduced English, embedding, constructions with prepositions; ASL use of space (establishing a referent); use of eye gaze; ASL pronouns and determiners, classifier predicates; discourse markers; idiosyncratic, "doubles"

oriented toward the forehead. However, it is a sign for the English word *because*, and its meaning and function are those of the English word. ASL does have conjunctions but this is not one of them. The ASL conjunction used in a situation in which English uses *because* might be WHY or REASON, with very specific nonmanual signals. Other examples of ASL-like signs that occur in contact signing include signs for English prepositions such as TO, ON, IN, BEHIND, and UNDER. Again, these signs are composed of the same parts from which ASL signs are composed, but their meaning and function cannot be said to be ASL. In the first place, ASL accomplishes the kind of grammatical relationships that prepositions accomplish with a category of signs called classifier predicates. Second, in the contact signing we observed, these signs for prepositions occur in sentences with English word order or in English collocations, such as DEPEND ON, MORE ATTENTION ON, GIVE MORE MEANING TO, GIVE ME TIME TO, and IN THE FIRST PLACE. These signs are interesting because any member of the Deaf community is able to produce "the ASL sign for *on*," for example, but these signs for English prepositions cannot be said to be part of the grammar of ASL. We will recall that a number of methodical signs were devised at the Hartford school to represent parts of English in the same way that methodical signs had been invented to represent parts of French. This led us to our earlier suggestion in Chapter 1 that these signs for English prepositions (and perhaps other signs for English words such as AND and FOR) have been around for a long time, having been devised in or around 1817. It is also important to note that we make a distinction between ASL-like signs and the signs which have been invented to manually code English, many of which clearly violate the morpheme structure conditions of ASL in a variety of ways. For example, in signs in which both hands move, ASL signs generally require that the handshape of both hands be identical; in signs which have different handshapes, there is a fairly limited number of handshapes acceptable for the passive or base hand. However, signs in the systems invented to manually code English often violate these constraints (Baker, 1990).

   We say that most of the lexical forms in contact signing are ASL signs and ASL-like signs. Contact signing also has English lexical items produced in two different ways: (1) single, isolated mouthed or audibly spoken English words with no accompanying signs, and (2) mouthing or whispering of English words with accompanying signs. An example of the first is in clip #2, in which the informant stops signing and says the English word *so;* the informant in clip #14 signs IN and WAY and speaks the word *a* with no sign, so the result is IN "a" WAY.[8] Isolated words may also occur without voice, as in clip #15. The informant mouths the English words *or, I, to, the, is,* and *don't* with no accompanying signs. As concerns mouthing with accompanying signs, we can say that it is a central feature of contact signing. In describing language contact phenomena in ASL interpretation, Davis (1989) draws a distinction between full English mouthing and reduced English mouthing. The former consists of the complete pronunciation of the word, generally without voice. The latter consists of the partial pronunciation of the word, still without voice. Both of these phenomena are different from two other phenomena. One is what Davis calls lexicalized mouthing, that is, a severely reduced mouthing of the English word which accompanies the ASL sign. For example, the mouth configuration which accompanies the sign FINISH clearly has its origin in the articulation of the spoken English word *finish;* likewise the mouth configuration of the sign HAVE. Another phenomenon is the mouth configuration that may accompany an ASL sign but has nothing to do with spoken English. We discussed two examples of this in Chapter 1: the mouth configuration that is part of the sign FINALLY and the one that is part of the sign formed with a 4 handshape that closes as it moves across the chin, palm facing in, and that can be glossed as WELL-I'LL-BE-DARNED. Both of these can be considered integral parts of the individual lexical items they accompany. But one of the distinguishing features of contact signing is mouthing which ranges from full pronunciation to reduced mouthing. It is distinct from lexicalized mouthing in that it is continuously produced during an utterance or turn. It is not restricted to individual isolated lexical items. ASL may sometimes have instances of lexicalized or full mouthing within a clearly ASL discourse and we do not want to suggest that there is never full mouthing in ASL. This notwithstanding Schermer's (1990) reading of our findings:

---

8. A transcript of each clip is provided in Appendix II. The clips are numbered according to the first order in which they occurred on the judgment tape. Their order in the appendix reflects the order in which they are discussed.

> Lucas and Valli (1989) define mouthing of English words as part of contact signing or signed English. According to them it should not be considered part of ASL. Even in cases where native users do not recognize mouthing as a phonological remnant of English the mouthing is considered to be part of contact signing rather than ASL. Davis suggests that some English words are lexicalized into ASL, while Lucas and Valli consider mouthing as typical or contact-language thus suggesting that mouthing should not be considered part of ASL. [pp. 148–149]

We *never* made these claims or suggestions and clearly we recognize lexicalized mouthing (and occasional full mouthing) as part of ASL, even though the result of language contact. We simply want to distinguish between the kind of mouthing that occurs during the production of ASL and the kind that occurs during the production of contact signing, a distinction that seems justified. The major distinction between mouthing in ASL and mouthing in contact signing is one of mouthing of isolated items (be it full or reduced or lexicalized) with morphological and syntactic structure that is clearly ASL versus *continuous* mouthing accompanying a grammatical structure that, as we shall see, combines elements of both English and ASL. The contact signing mouthing is also distinct from what we call Sign-Supported Speech (Signed English, for example) in two ways: (1) It is generally voiceless, while SSS is usually audibly spoken English with accompanying signs; and (2) whether it is voiced or voiceless (or in the case of clip #6, whispered), it does not include the mouthing of bound English morphemes (and their respective allomorphs) such as plural -*s*, possessive -*s*, third person singular -*s*, past tense -*ed*, progressive -*ing*, and so forth. In fact, in the two clips in which the informants' voices are audible, an examination of what they are voicing reveals that they are "speaking contact signing." That is, they are producing English words with their mouths but the structure of what they are signing (and hence voicing or whispering) combines elements of ASL and English structure. It cannot be said to be Sign-Supported Speech. We suggest that this kind of mouthing is a representation of English lexical items unique to the ASL–English contact situation. The forms are clearly a kind of English—they are not signs, the hands are not involved. It is interesting to notice that sometimes the signs produced by the hands and the mouthing don't exactly match. We noticed at least three examples of this: in clip #7, in which the informant signs DOESN'T-MATTER and mouths "even though" (the argument could probably be made here that "even though" is a reasonable translation of the sign DOESN'T-MATTER, but what's interesting is that the informant does not mouth "doesn't matter" even though it would be appropriate.); in clip #19, in which the informant signs NONE and mouths "have no"; and in the same clip, in which the informant signs INFORM-third person and mouths "thank you." And if the mouthing is voiceless, as it is in six of the nine clips, it clearly reflects the element of deafness, either because of the stigma placed on using one's voice (often viewed negatively because of the traditional role of oralism in deaf education to the express exclusion of ASL) or because the signer knows that a Deaf cointerlocutor can't hear the voice and therefore cannot benefit from it, or both. What is very interesting to notice is that the clips in which the informant mouths with voice (#6, 14, and 19) are taken from portions of the interviews with the Deaf interviewer, and presumably the informant knows that the Deaf interviewer can't hear the voice. This points to sociolinguistic explanations, as opposed to purely audiological ones, for the occurrence of mouthing with voice. That is, contact signing with voice may be seen as most appropriate for formal interview-type situations, regardless of the audiological status of the other participants.

Our data provide examples of all of these phenomena. We of course see examples of lexicalized mouth configurations and of ASL mouth configurations, since many of the lexical forms are ASL forms. But we also see many examples of the full and reduced mouthing typical of contact signing. As can be seen from the transcripts, many informants produce continual voiceless mouthing, as in clips #2, 3, 7, 8, 15, and 20. Some of it is relatively full mouthing, as in clip #3:

+MOUTHING ———————————————————————————————————————→

BUT   HAVE   A   PERSON   WHO   QUALIFY   ENOUGH

Some of it is more reduced, as with the informant in clip #2, who fingerspells #ED ("education") and mouths "educa-". Figure 7 shows a portion of clip #2 and provides an example of the almost continuous voiceless mouthing typical of contact signing.

+ MOUTHING ─────────→

neg   _neg_

PRO-1   AGREE   PRO-1   AGREE THAT BECAUSE   PRO:1

─────────────────→

brow up   _gaze center_   _gaze center_

SUPPORT DEAF INSTITUTION BECAUSE PRO:3-center MORE

─────────────────────→

gaze center

ATTENTION ON SPECIFIC #OF LIFE STYLE AND PRO:3-center

+ MOUTHING ─────────────────────→

gaze center   _gaze center_

MORE GENERAL GOOD #ED DEPEND ON WHAT STATE WHICH

─────────────────────→

PLACE HAVE BEST DEPEND ON PEOPLE'S EXPERIENCE "WELL"

+ MOUTHING ─────────→ "so" + MOUTHING ─────────→

gaze center

BACKGROUND #OF TEACH ING   COOPERATIVE TEAM WORK

─────────────────→

gaze center

#IS REAL MOST KEY THEIR #GOALS ETC (nodding head) #OK

'I don't agree with that because I support deaf residential schools because they place more attention on the specifics of lifestyle and the education, in general, is better—depending on what state, which place has the best—that depends on the people's experience, on their teaching background—so, cooperative teamwork is really the key to their goals, OK.'

Figure 7 A portion of clip #2 shows the nearly continuous voiceless mouthing that is typical of contact signing.

Lexical Meaning and Function

Although most of the lexical forms are ASL signs with ASL meaning and function, sometimes the lexical forms have English meanings and functions, and some are idiosyncratic. For example, the ASL sign GROW (the sign used when discussing the growth of plants, for example) is produced by one informant with the lexicalized fingerspelled sign #UP in a discussion of the hearing children of deaf parents. Even though the sign GROW used by the informant is an ASL sign, it is not the sign typically used in ASL for talking about the growth of children. The result, then, is the use of an ASL form with a meaning not usually associated with that sign. This example is analogous to examples in the various manual codes for English, where one ASL sign is used for a wide variety of English meanings, even though separate ASL signs exist for those meanings. For example, the ASL sign RUN (as in "run down the street") is cited in these systems for the meanings of "run for president," "run a business," or "run in a stocking." The occurrence of the sign GROW with the fingerspelled #UP may be a reflection of the signer's exposure to manually coded systems for English in the educational system. And in a situation deemed appropriate for more English-like signing, evidence of those systems emerges. GROW, then, is a case of an ASL sign that is not being used with its ASL meaning. In that usage, it has an English meaning. And the verb phrase GROW #UP is also an example of an ASL loan translation. It is interesting that the loan translation, with its two separate signs, reflects the structure of the English verb phrase. As we mentioned earlier, there exists another ASL sign, completely different in form, for talking about the growth and growing up of children.

Another example in the data of ASL lexical forms with English meaning and function is the sign MEAN, which in ASL is generally used as a verb, as in

WH
_____

WORD   MEAN

"What does the word mean?" In the data, however, this sign occurs with the meaning and function of the English noun *meaning*, as in the sequence WHAT MEAN OF QUOTE DEAF CULTURE, "What is the meaning of 'deaf culture'?" One other example occurs in clip #7, in which the informant signs this sequence:

REALLY MAKE IMP- BIG IMPACT INFLUENCE DEAF HEARING

PEOPLE

Generally the sign IMPACT is an agreement verb in ASL, in which location and orientation indicate the subject and the object. In this case, however, it occurs in the phrase MAKE BIG IMPACT and functions as a noun.

This sequence also provides an example of an idiosyncratic use of a sign, a meaning and function that is not quite English and not quite ASL. That is the sign INFLUENCE. In ASL, this is an agreement verb like IMPACT in which palm orientation and location indicate the subject and the object. Generally, the object would be introduced into the discourse and the verb would then be oriented toward the point in space indicating the referent of the object. The word order would be DEAF HEARING PEOPLE INFLUENCE. In English, the word *influence* can function either as a noun or as a verb. As a noun, it can occur in a variety of phrases such as "exert influence" or "have influence." It cannot occur with the verb *make*, however, as in "make influence." In this sequence, MAKE INFLUENCE is not English; the word order of INFLUENCE DEAF HEARING PEOPLE is not ASL. It would appear, then, that the sign INFLUENCE has an idiosyncratic meaning and function.

Morphological Structure

In our preliminary description of the features of contact signing (Lucas and Valli, 1989), we had characterized the morphological structure of contact signing as "reduced ASL and English, reduction and/or absence of nonmanual signals . . . English inflectional and derivational morphology is nonexistent, yielding a very analytic (as opposed to synthetic) picture" (p. 30). Further analysis has led us to revise this characterization somewhat. The analysis of the nine contact signing clips still reveals drastically reduced ASL and English morphology, but it is not completely absent. For example, we find some fingerspelled signs for English inflectional and derivational morphemes, such as #ING and #MENT. And we find some examples of inflected ASL verbs, as in the following segment from clip #8:

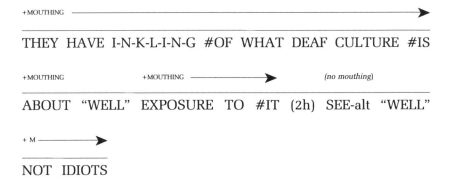

NOT IDIOTS

'They have an inkling of what deaf culture is about, exposure to it. They have seen it for a long time. They are not idiots.'

In this example, the informant uses an inflected form of the ASL sign SEE. This inflected form is a two-handed sign with a V handshape, produced in alternating elliptical circles away from the signer's face. It can be glossed as SEE FOR A LONG TIME. It is important to notice that during the production of this sign the mouthing stops and resumes following the sign "WELL." There are many other examples in the data. In clip #15, the following sequence occurs (which is a part of a sentence):

CAN-BE ANY ONE DEAF "or" HEARING DOESN'T-MATTER

The informant mouths English words for every sign through the sign HEARING. She mouths the English word *or* with no sign. And she stops mouthing and produces the ASL sign DOESN'T MATTER. She immediately resumes mouthing after this sign. In clip #19, the informant uses five different inflected ASL verbs—INFORM, MEET, TELL, WARN, and COME-UP-TO—all verbs that use location and orientation morphemically. In some cases, the verb is used as it is in ASL but is embedded in an English phrase, as follows:

+MOUTHING ———— "have no" ————————————————————→

MANY "of" US NONE TIME "to" WARN++ WHO RIGHT PERSON

'Many of us don't have the time to warn a lot of [hearing people] as to who the appropriate person to help us.'

In this case, the English words *of, have,* and *to* are mouthed without accompanying signs. The word *no* is mouthed with the sign NONE. The verb WARN is produced away from the signer in a space that might indicate a third person object, as opposed to being signed near the signer with a different palm orientation, indicating a first-person subject. The verb WARN here is inflected not only for third person but also for distributive aspect. That is, it is repeated three times, each time in a location adjacent to the previous one, with the meaning of "warn many people." The word order in which the verb occurs, however, is basically English, particularly the use of the relative pronoun WHO. This kind of embedding of inflected ASL verbs also occurs with TELL, INFORM, and COME-UP-TO (produced as a classifier predicate with a 1 handshape, hence 1-CL). For example, this sequence occurs:

+MOUTHING   (no mouthing)   + MOUTHING ————————→
                                                                  cond

...FIND DEAF 1-CL COME-UP-TO-PRO.1 HELP, FINE NOT

+MOUTHING ————————————→

NEED #IT, TELL-PRO:3 NONE

+MOUTHING ———————————————————— "thank you" ————————→
              "don't"

THANK-YOU   NEED YOUR HELP BUT INFORM PRO:3

'[A hearing person] discovers that you're deaf and approaches you to offer help. Fine. If that's not necessary, tell them "No, thank you, I don't need your help but thank you anyway." '

COME-UP-TO is a classifier predicate with a 1 hand-shape. In this example, the signer moves the hand toward her face, to mean that a hearing person has approached her. The mouthing produced all the way through the sequence stops during the production of the verb COME-UP-TO and then resumes immediately. The verb TELL is inflected to show a third-person object, as is the verb INFORM, which is produced while the informant says "Thank you" in English.

Interestingly, while inflected ASL verbs do occur, we also see examples of verbs that can be inflected in ASL but are not in these data. An example occurs in clip #19 with the verb HELP. In the sequence COME-UP-TO HELP, the sign HELP could indicate subject and object with location, but does not.

In our preliminary analysis, we had said "reduction and/or absence of nonmanual signals," but we find some clear examples of ASL nonmanual signals in these clips. In clip #2, the informant signs

neg

PRO.1 AGREE PRO.1 AGREE

'I don't agree.'

The designation *neg* indicates the shaking of the head, an ASL negation marker. In clip #15, we see the following:

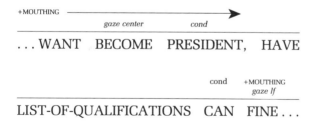

+MOUTHING ———————————————————————▶
                gaze center   *cond*

... WANT   BECOME   PRESIDENT,   HAVE

                              cond   +MOUTHING
                                        gaze lf

LIST-OF-QUALIFICATIONS   CAN   FINE ...

'[If the person] wants to become president and has the qualifications and is able, fine.'

In this example, we see the nonmanual signal for conditionals occurring with the sequence WANT BECOME PRESIDENT and with the sign CAN—raised eyebrows and head tilted forward. This informant also uses the negation marker. Another informant signs

+MOUTHING ——————— "That is"   rhet +MOUTHING ——————————▶

PRO.1   THINK   BECAUSE   WHY   WE   WON'T   BITE   PRO:2

'I think because we won't bite you.'

The sign WHY here is a rhetorical question in ASL, used as a conjunction, and has a particular nonmanual signal: raised eyebrows. The head may also be slightly tilted. This is also an example of what we call "doubles" in the data, of which we have more than one example. Doubles are cases in which the same grammatical feature is produced in both a signed representation of English and in ASL and mouthed simultaneously. In this case, the sign BECAUSE reflects English structure, while the sign WHY with its nonmanual marker is part of ASL structure with the same function of the English conjunction *because*. Another example occurred with a conditional construction:

cond   +m ————————————————▶
gaze down   "I am"   *gaze down*

#IF   MOTIVATED   PRO:1   SURE   GUARANTEE   PRO:3   LEARN,

neg
gaze down ————————

BUT MOTIVATED

'If they were motivated, I guarantee for sure that they would learn but they're just not motivated.'[9]

In this case, the fingerspelled sign #IF is part of ASL but it is not necessary to mark a conditional. This can be done with raised eyebrows and a tilted head, as we see with the sign MOTIVATED. We suggest that the use of the sign #IF here is reflective of English structure, so that the sentence is doubly marked for conditional. Notice also that the negative nonmanual also occurs here.

9. This clip is not one of the nine.

This description of the occurrence of inflected ASL verbs and ASL nonmanual signals raises the questions of whether these are best described as part of contact signing or whether they represent switches to ASL during a contact signing discourse. We will return to these questions in a later section.

Syntactic Structure

In our 1989 description, we said that the syntactic structure of contact signing consisted of reduced English syntax with some idiosyncratic constructions. Analysis of our data has revealed the situation to be somewhat more complex. As can be seen from Table 7, English features found in the clips include prepositions, constructions with *that*, verbs with particles, relative clauses, modals, conjunctions, comparative *more,* and collocations. Many of the sentences follow English word order, but there are also some idiosyncratic syntactic constructions, constructions that fit neither the ASL nor the English grammatical system. Examples include sequences such as

+MOUTHING ──────────────▶
_____

GROW #UP OF #BE DEAF

and

+MOUTHING ───────────────────────────────────────▶
_____

COOPERATIVE   TEAMWORK   #IS   REAL   MOST   KEY

+MOUTHING ─────────▶
_____

THEIR #GOALS

and

+MOUTHING ───────────────────────────────────────▶
_____

THEY   HAVE   I-N-K-L-I-N-G   #OF   WHAT   DEAF   CULTURE

_____

#IS   ABOUT

What we had not focused on in our earlier analysis is the presence in all of the clips of a significant number of ASL syntactic features, such as the use of eye gaze and body shifting and the use of pronouns, determiners, classifier predicates, and ASL discourse markers. In addition, four informants also establish topics in the signing space—for example, residential schools on the right and mainstreaming programs on the left—and then consistently refer to them throughout the discourse using English syntactic constructions. This does not occur in the nine clips, however, and we will return to discussion of it in a later section. We include it in our inventory in Table 7 (ASL use of space) because even though there was a lot of disagreement among the judges as to the status of the four clips in which it occurred, the master judgments and our analysis clearly show these clips not to be ASL and we are comfortable calling them contact signing.

As we shall see, some of these syntactic features necessarily occur sequentially but some of them occur simultaneously with English syntactic constructions and English mouthing. There are many instances of ASL pronouns in the clips, such as PRO:1 ("I"), PRO:2 ("You"), and PRO:3 ("he", "she," or "it"). These are important to notice because the informants sometimes use the fingerspelled pronouns devised in manual codes for English such as #HE or #THEM or the sign I used in these codes. Some informants even alternate between the ASL pronoun and the manually coded English pronoun in the same clip. Clip #7 has examples of determiners, as in the sequence

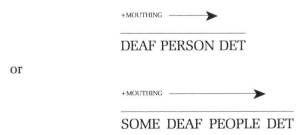

DEAF PERSON DET

or

SOME DEAF PEOPLE DET

'The deaf person'; 'Some deaf people'

The discourse marker that we noticed can be glossed as WELL or YOU-KNOW and seems to have the function of making sure that the cointerlocutor is following the discourse or of a pause marker, as in this sequence from clip #6:

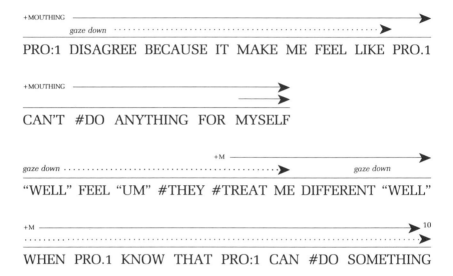

'I disagree because it makes me feel like I can't do anything for myself—well, um, I feel, um, they treat me differently—well—when I know that I can do something.'

Woodward and Markowicz (1975), in their inventory of PSE features, include English word order and the absence of determiners. We find evidence of the former, but while we find no fingerspelled signs for English determiners such as #THE, we do see plenty of ASL determiners. And clearly there are many other features in these data that are not found in their inventory. To fully understand what kind of phenomenon contact signing is, it is useful to compare it to (1) inventories of the features of English-based spoken language pidgins, and (2) features of other kinds of signing such as Signed English, which by its very nature is English based. We presented such a comparison in 1989, and we re-present it here in Table 10, based on our current understanding of contact signing. We can see that contact signing is quite distinct from Signed English, and with our identification of many ASL features in contact signing, we find

10. The informant mouthed almost all of the way through this sequence.

Table 10

Comparison of Linguistic Features among Various Systems

Features	Spoken English	ASL	Signed English	Contact signing	English-based spoken language pidgins (based on Mühlhäusler, 1986)
Lexical form	English	ASL	ASL, ASL-like signs, non-ASL-like signs, spoken English	ASL and ASL-like signs, English whispering and mouthing, single spoken words	English, some substrate, some idiosyncratic
Lexical function and meaning	English	ASL	English	ASL, idiosyncratic, English	Usually English, some idiosyncratic
Morphology	English	ASL	Reduced English and ASL, signed representation of bound morphemes	Reduced ASL and English, some signs for English morphemes, some ASL inflected verbs and nonmanual signals	Reduced English
Syntax	English	ASL	Reduced English	Reduced English, embedding, constructions with prepositions, some idiosyncratic constructions, ASL use of space, eyegaze, pronouns, determiners, discourse markers, reduced use of classifier predicates	Basically SVO, reduced use of pronouns and prepositions, embedding rare

it is even more different from English-based spoken language pidgins than we originally thought. Specifically, if the pidgin analogy has ASL as the substrate, then the substrate in this case contributes a fairly large number of morphological and syntactic features, which is usually not the case in spoken language pidgins. Not that pidgins never have significant features from the substrate. For example, Tok Pisin has a first-person inclusive plural and a first-person exclusive plural, a highly marked feature from the Austronesian substrate (Romaine, 1988). Furthermore, the lexical forms in contact signing are *signs,* as well as mouthing, whispering, and single spoken English words. In spoken language pidgins, most (not all) of the lexical forms are from the superstrate. The lexical function and meaning of contact signing forms is ASL, English, and sometimes idiosyncratic, which does not differ from spoken language pidgins except that it would appear that in spoken language pidgins the main lexical function and meaning are from the superstrate (e.g., English), and that substrate or idiosyncratic function and meaning occur to a lesser degree. Spoken language pidgins are characterized by reduced morphologies, for example, no distinctions of gender or case and elimination of agreement markers. In contact signing we see some signs for English-bound morphemes, some ASL inflected verbs, and nonmanual signals which serve morphological functions. Romaine (1988) remarks that pidgin syntax is "shallow . . . Pidgins lack rules for embedding and subordination of clauses. They tend to use no formal marking to indicate that one part of an utterance is subordinate to another. Distinctive marking of relative clauses comes later in the stabilization or expansion phase of the pidgin life cycle, or arises in the process of creolization" (p. 241). However, in contact signing we see some English relative clauses, extensive use of prepositional phrases, as well as ASL syntactic features such as establishing a topic in space, eye gaze, pronouns, determiners, and discourse markers. In 1989, we said that contact signing combines ASL and ASL-like lexical items in a reduced English syntactic system. At this point, the data reveal that the morphological and syntactic system of contact signing cannot simply be characterized as "reduced English" or as a pidgin. Sociolinguistically, it does not fit the criteria for defining pidgins, either. Let us assume, for the sake of analogy, that English is considered the superstrate language in the Deaf community. Clearly it is the native language of hearing users of contact signing. But even Deaf native ASL signers, for whom English may not be a native language, have extensive exposure to and contact with English in various forms, first in educational settings and later in their adult lives through employment, interaction with hearing people, and print and broadcast media. This exposure to and contact with English is accompanied by ongoing ASL interaction with other native signers. The result does not match the situations in which pidgins have been said to arise. It is a maintained bilingualism, one outcome of which is contact signing.

"So If It's Not a Pidgin, What Is It?"

We come finally to the question of "How *do* we want to characterize contact signing?" The short answer is that we are dealing with what Romaine (1989) refers to as a "third system" phenomenon, "the outcome of contact between two systems" which "must be analyzed in terms of its own structure rather than in terms of one language or the other" (p. 147). Also of relevance here is Grosjean's (1992) observation that, according to a

> wholistic view . . . the bilingual is a fully competent speaker–hearer; he or she has developed competencies (in the two languages and possibly in a third system that is a combination of the first two) to the extent required by his or her needs and those of the environment. The bilingual uses the two languages—separately or together—for different purposes, in different domains of life, with different people. [in press]

Contact signing appears to be somewhat analogous to the cocoliche described by Whinnom (1971), the Spanish spoken by Italian immigrants in Argentina (but not spoken by Argentines). After introducing the notion of linguistic hybridization, he (1971, p. 97) observes:

> It is a now despised formula of "primitive" creolistics that pidgin is made up of the vocabulary of one language and the grammar of another. The observation may be faulty but it reflects a basic reality. It is, moreover, a description which fits very well certain linguistic phenomena ("secondary languages") associated with naive language learning.

At the least intense level of hybridization that he describes, Spanish lexical items (nouns, adjectives, verb radicals) are imported into an

Italian morphosyntactic system without interfering with the native phonological system. It could be referred to as code-mixing, but it is a kind of code mixing that is quite different than that described thus far for spoken languages. In Chapter 1, we reviewed different definitions of code switching and code mixing for spoken languages. Central to understanding both code switching and code mixing in spoken languages is that even though the parts of two different codes can be switched intersententially or mixed intrasententially, the switching or mixing is sequential in nature, as opposed to being simultaneous. That is, units in spoken languages, whether phonological, morphological, or syntactic, are necessarily produced one after the other. If, in a code mixing situation, the verb of one language is marked with an inflection from another language, this event is also sequential, that is, first the verb is produced, followed by the inflection. In spoken language situations, speakers have at their disposal the phonological, morphological, syntactic, and discourse components of two or more languages, and it is possible to imagine a simultaneous mix of, say, the phonology of one language with the morphology of another, or the morphology of one with the syntax of another. It seems, however, that mixing *within* components, while possible, is necessarily sequential. That is, it seems impossible to simultaneously produce two phonological events from two different spoken languages. In the contact signing that we are describing, however, in which a signer produces ASL lexical items on the hands and simultaneously mouths the corresponding English lexical items, the result is the simultaneous production of two separate codes. The situation is made more complex by the fact that the ASL lexical items being produced with the hands may occur in a combination of English syntactic structure and ASL syntactic structure. As we said, we see clear evidence of English structure in the use of prepositional phrases, conjunctions, and relative clauses. The basic word order is subject-verb-object (SVO). While ASL and English have this basic word order in common, it is not the most frequently used word order in ASL, with the use of topicalization being more frequent, for example. But we saw very few examples of topicalization in the clips, and while we saw some ASL nonmanual syntactic markers such as yes–no questions, rhetorical questions, conditionals, and negatives, we saw no nonmanual topic or relative clause markers. However, we do see ASL pronouns, determiners, and classifier predicates, the use of points in the signing space to establish topics, the use of eye gaze and body shifting, and the use of ASL discourse markers. Some of these ASL syntactic features necessarily occur sequentially—that is, a topic must be established at a point in space *before* it can be talked about using whatever structure. So in that case, an ASL syntactic device occurs before one that reflects English syntactic structure. We will provide examples of this in a later section. But some of the ASL syntactic features, such as pronouns, determiners, eye gaze, and body shifting, occur with English mouthing. In clip #7, for example, the informant produces this sequence while mouthing English:

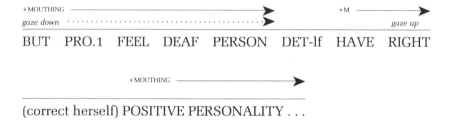

(correct herself) POSITIVE PERSONALITY . . .

'But I feel [if] the deaf person has the right . . . positive personality. . .'

The ASL pronoun PRO.1 occurs simultaneously with the English mouthing of "I". The determiner is an index finger immediately following the sign PERSON and pointing to the right. The informant does not mouth the English word *the,* so *the* and the ASL determiner do not occur simultaneously, but the ASL determiner does occur as all of the other signs are being mouthed. The same informant produces this sequence:

WOW   REALLY   MAKE   IMP . . . BIG IMPACT . . .

'I . . . from my experience I know those deaf people who, even though it's through an interpreter, really make a big impact . . .'

The informant also mouths all the way through this sequence, except for signs WOW, REALLY, and IMPACT. In fact, the informant signs DOESN'T-MATTER and mouths "even though," further evidence of the simultaneous occurence of ASL lexical items and English mouthing.

Finally, we see cases in which ASL is produced on one hand and contact signing is produced on the other, as in this sequence:

Right hand

           +MOUTHING   +MOUTHING   ⟶

ONE   FRIEND   PRO.3   HEARING   PRO.3   #ADOPT   #BY   DEAF

⟶

PARENTS   PRO.3

Left hand

1-CL: PERSON ⟶

'One hearing friend, he was adopted by deaf parents.'

In this example, the informant starts out with ONE FRIEND and then uses an ASL third-person pronoun and indicates the classifier predicate being produced with the left hand. (1-CL: PERSON is the classifier predicate produced with a 1 handshape.) It represents the friend in question, and the use of that predicate is a feature of ASL. The left hand producing the classifier predicate stays in place while the right hand produces the sequence #ADOPT BY DEAF PARENTS PRO.3. The use of the prepositional phrase BY DEAF PARENTS is not ASL, but the repetition of the third-person pronoun is acceptable in ASL structure. This segment has a structure that sequentially combines elements of ASL and English. We also see the simultaneous production of an ASL classifier predicate on the left hand and the mouthing of the words *hearing* and *adopt by deaf parents.*

What we seem to see, then, is a system that combines elements from the phonological, morphological, syntactic, and discourse components of English and ASL, often allowing the simultaneous production of elements within the same component. The most useful analogy seems to be the convergence situation described by Gumperz and Wilson (1971), in which a single syntactic surface structure is the result of the extended contact among three languages.[11]

One question that comes up is whether the occurrence of ASL features should be described as part of contact signing or whether their occurrence should be described as switches to ASL. We suggest that the ASL elements that we have described so far are indeed part of contact signing and that they can be clearly distinguished from switches to ASL, of which we have examples in the data. For example, in clip #3, the informant produces this sequence:

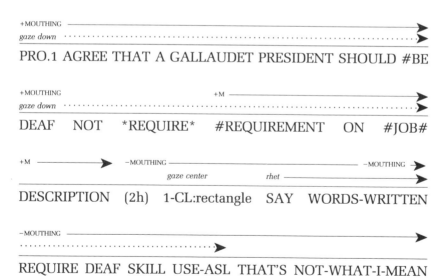

+MOUTHING ⟶
gaze down ⟶

PRO.1 AGREE THAT A GALLAUDET PRESIDENT SHOULD #BE

+MOUTHING   +M ⟶
gaze down

DEAF   NOT   *REQUIRE*   #REQUIREMENT   ON   #JOB#

+M ⟶   −MOUTHING ⟶   −MOUTHING ⟶
         gaze center   *rhet* ⟶

DESCRIPTION   (2h)   1-CL:rectangle   SAY   WORDS-WRITTEN

−MOUTHING ⟶

REQUIRE DEAF SKILL USE-ASL THAT'S NOT-WHAT-I-MEAN

11. It may be that some spoken language contact situations result in the simultaneous production of features from different phonological systems within a given phonological segment, thus accounting for certain accents. Contact signing is still unique, because we see the simultaneous production of *whole* phonological segments from English and ASL.

+MOUTHING ——▶
    gaze down ··▶

BUT   HAVE   PERSON   WHO   QUALIFY   ENOUGH   HAPPEN

–MOUTHING ————▶

DEAF   FINE

'I agree that the president of Gallaudet should be deaf; not that it should be a requirement
on the job description, like "the applicant must be a skilled ASL user"—that's not what
I mean. But if there's a person who's qualified enough who happens to be deaf, fine.'

In the first part of this sequence, the informant mouths, and we can
see a construction with *that* and the fingerspelled sign for the English word *be*, and it is clearly contact signing. The informant then
stops mouthing, moves her body slightly forward and turns to the
left, and beginning with the sign SAY, signs ASL. This continues
until the sign BUT, at which point she resumes mouthing and the
structure is again contact signing, with an English-like relative
clause. We see the sequence between SAY and BUT as a shift to
ASL. For example, the whole sequence SAY WORDS-WRITTEN
REQUIRE DEAF SKILL USE-ASL is produced with raised eyebrows, the nonmanual signal used for rhetorical questions, and
could be translated as "Should it say on the application that a deaf
skilled ASL user is required?" Furthermore, the sign glossed as
WORDS-WRITTEN is produced with the palm toward the other
signer, that is, it shows agreement with the object, as if the signer
were being shown the job description. Finally, the syntactic structure of this sequence is not English and there is no mouthing. The
moving forward of the body and the slight turn to the left seem to
flag a shift to ASL and we see this with other informants who shift
to ASL. For example, in clip #16, when talking about black deaf
children having a hard time learning English and trying to get the
attention of their white teacher, the informant produces contact
signing while mouthing, as follows:

+MOUTHING ——▶
                 gaze down

. . . NOT LOOK-left BLACK TRY HARD WITH THAT ENGLISH

and then shifts to ASL without mouthing:

gaze up ——————————————⟶ gaze down ——————————————⟶
    take role of student   *take role of teacher*

/CALL-ON-TEACHER INSIST/PRO.3 (teacher)/HOLD-ON QUICK-

gaze down ——————————————————————————⟶

EXPLANATION SHORT FINISH SHORT KEEP-DISTANCE . . .

With the signs CALL-ON-TEACHER INSIST, the informant's eye gaze is up, taking the role of a child talking to a teacher; beginning with the sign PRO.3, the eye gaze is down, taking the role of a teacher responding to a child. Again, the syntactic structure is clearly ASL, and we are treating this as a shift to ASL. The main criterion for distinguishing between a feature of ASL that is part of contact signing and a shift to ASL is size: We have many examples of single isolated ASL items that occur within more English-like syntactic structure, such as inflected verbs, pronouns, determiners, and examples of ASL syntactic features such as the establishment of topics in the signing space that precede more English-like syntactic structure. These isolated features are distinct from ASL phrases or sentences (or in some cases, paragraphs), which are most often flagged by body shifting and eye gaze not accompanied by mouthing and whose internal structure is ASL. It is interesting to note that many of the latter are examples of constructed dialogue (Tannen, 1986) in which someone is quoted or a conversation is reproduced. As concerns the isolated ASL features, Romaine (1989) remarks that "a related problem in distinguishing between borrowing and code-switching is the extent to which it is possible to assign a base language to a stretch of bilingual discourse" (p. 134). We suggest that these isolated ASL items do not constitute switches to ASL, but rather are part of the structure of contact signing. This is easy to prove in the case of inflected ASL verbs, pronouns, determiners, and nonmanual signals that occur with mouthing or as part of English constructions such as prepositional phrases or relative clauses. But it would be hard to justify as *switches* to ASL even the relatively small number of isolated items that occur without mouthing and are not embedded in English structure. We suggest that they are clearly ASL items that occur as a part of contact signing. That is, there is such a thing as contact signing discourse, a third system which bilinguals have at their disposal, and it includes the use of individual ASL features such as inflected verbs, pronouns, determiners, and so forth. These isolated individual items are clearly different from stretches of ASL discourse which show ASL syntactic structure and most often are flagged by body shifting.

Discussion of a third system brings us to the videotaped clips about which there was marked disagreement among the judges. They include clips #4, 5, 11, 13, and 16. As we mentioned earlier, they were not included among the nine clips that we have analyzed so far, mainly because there was less than an 85% rate of agreement between the judges and the master judgments. However, an analysis of these clips shows two interesting things. One is that even though many of the judges judged these clips to be ASL, their structure is what we have described as contact signing. The second is that they all share two ASL features that may account for the judgments of these clips as ASL. Tables 11 and 12 present a comparison of the clips for which there was an 85% or better rate of agreement with those for which there was disagreement in terms of presence of English and ASL features. In Table 11, we see that all of the clips for which there was agreement have conjunctions, mouthing, and English word order, and almost all have prepositions. This is also true of the clips for which there was disagreement, except for the absence of conjunctions in clips #11 and 16. The clips for which there was agreement also show some English features lacking in the disagreement ones, such as comparative *more*, relative clauses, and constructions with *that*. But in terms of English features, we can't say that there is much difference between agreement and disagreement clips. The real difference can be seen in Table 10, where we see that four of the disagreement clips (#4, 5, 11, and 16) all use ASL eye gaze and the ASL syntactic structure of establishing a topic at points in the signing space and then consistently referring to those points. One informant sets up mainstreaming on the left and residential schools on the right and then discusses each with contact signing while turning the body and the eye gaze to the relevant point. The result is contact signing on the hands with its combination of English and ASL features, simultaneously produced with ASL body and eye gaze shifting. Three

TABLE 11
English Features in Contact Sign Segments

English features	2	3	6	7	8	14	15	19	20	Alone	4	5	11	16	Alone	13	Proportion
Clip condition	H[a]	D	D	Alone	H	D	H	D	Alone		D	H	Alone	Alone		Alone	
Conjunctions (and, because, but)	✓	✓	✓	✓	✓	✓	✓	✓	✓	9/9	✓	✓			2/4	✓	12/14
Prepositions	✓	✓	✓	✓	✓		✓		✓	7/9	✓	✓	✓	✓	4/4		11/14
Verb with prepositions	✓	✓								2/9		✓		✓	2/4		4/14
Invented Morphemes (#ING; #BE; IT; I; #MENT; #ED, 2 hands)	✓	✓							✓	3/9	✓	✓	✓	✓	4/4		7/14
Mouthing of English words	✓	✓	✓	✓	✓	✓	✓	✓	✓	9/9	✓	✓	✓	✓	4/4		13/14
English word order, collocations	✓	✓	✓	✓	✓	✓	✓	✓	✓	9/9	✓	✓	✓	✓	4/4	✓	14/14
Comparative *more* (vs. ASL intensifier)		✓							✓	2/9						✓	3/14
Relative clauses							✓			1/9							1/14
Determiners		✓			✓					2/9							2/14
Modal constructions	✓	✓								2/9							2/14
Contractions with *that* (subordinate clause)	✓	✓	✓				✓		✓	5/9	✓	✓			2/4		7/14
Unusual intialization (relatives)			✓							1/9							1/14
Proportion	8/12	10/12	6/12	4/12	5/12	3/12	6/12	3/12	7/12		6/12	7/12	4/12	5/12		3/12	

[a] H, with hearing interviewer; D, with Deaf interviewer; Alone, informants alone.

TABLE 12
ASL Features in Contact Sign Segments

English features	Clip# 2	3	6	7	8	14	15	19	20	Proportion	4	5	11	16	13	Proportion
	H[a]	D	D	Alone	H	D	H	D	Alone		D	H	Alone	Alone	Alone	
Nonmanual negation	✓				✓		✓			3/9					✓	4/14
Aspect			✓							1/9						1/14
Gaze										0/9	✓	✓	✓	✓		4/14
Pronouns	✓			✓	✓					3/9	✓	✓	✓	✓		7/14
Determiners				✓						1/9	✓					2/14
ASL word order										0/9						0/14
Conditional							✓			1/9					✓	2/14
Rhetorical question					✓					1/9			✓	✓		3/14
Topicalization										0/9			✓	✓		2/14
Lexical signs, no mouthing	✓	✓				✓	✓		✓	5/9	✓	✓				7/14
Locative verbs		✓						✓	✓	3/9						3/14
Agreement verbs				✓	✓			✓	✓	4/9				✓		5/14
Role shifting					✓					1/9						1/14
Discourse markers			✓		✓					2/9		✓				3/14
Proportion	3/14	2/14	2/14	3/14	5/14	2/14	3/14	2/14	3/14		4/14	4/14	4/14	5/14	2/14	

[a] H, with hearing interviewer; D, with Deaf interviewer; Alone, informants alone.

others do the same with black deaf students or black deaf education on one side and white deaf students or education on the other. Clip #13 is also a disagreement clip, but it differs from the others in that the disagreement is between white judges and black judges and not between community members and linguists and teachers, as with the other clips. Only 37% of the black judges said that this clip was not ASL (meaning 63% said that it was ASL), as opposed to 63% of white judges (community members and linguists and teachers combined) who said that it was not ASL. This clip has two ASL features, conditional and negation nonmanuals, but the word order cannot really be said to be ASL. The informant also does not mouth during this segment.

What is very interesting about these five segments is that even though their overall structure is that of contact signing, they share features that seem to result in judgments of the clips as ASL. This is particularly true of clips #4, 5, 11, and 16, which all have establishment of topic and the subsequent use of body shifting and eye gaze. And as we see from Table 10, those are both features absent from all of the clips for which there is agreement among the judges. We suggest that establishment of topic and use of body shifting and eye gaze are salient ASL features that carry a lot of weight, even if the overall structure of a clip cannot be said to be ASL. This brings to mind work by Graff, Labov, and Harris (1986) on two vowels in the phonology of the Philadelphia speech community: /aw/ and /ow/. Evidence from both production and perception in the community suggests that these two vowels are salient enough to be "recognized by white and black alike as markers of their respective speaking styles" (p. 57). Also of relevance is Gumperz's (1982) work on "contextualization cues" in discourse, the

> surface features of message form . . . by which speakers signal and listeners interpret what the activity is, how semantic content is to be understood and how each sentence relates to what precedes or follows . . . Roughly speaking, a contextualization cue is any feature of linguistic form that contributes to the signalling of contextual presuppositions. [p. 131]

The relevance of contextualization cues to our analysis is the significant work that may be done by a fairly subtle and discrete ASL linguistic item, even in the presence of many features that cannot be said to be ASL. Furthermore, since the overall structure of these five clips cannot be said to be ASL and is best described as contact signing, they provide even sharper evidence of a third system, even though the judgments of them were so varied.

We suggest, then, that contact signing is a third system resulting from the contact between ASL and English and consisting of features from both languages. We clearly don't want to call it a variety of English or a variety of ASL. We have been able to isolate and list features of English and ASL that consistently show up in the data, indicating the existence of a predictable and consistent system. That it is a system is further supported by the criterion of *intelligibility:* that is, the informants clearly understand each other and at no point in the data is there a communication breakdown attributable to the use of contact signing. It seems that intelligibility would be one important criterion for establishing the existence of a system and that the absence of a system would be indicated by breakdowns in communication. If what was being produced was not systematic and intelligible, presumably the receivers would react accordingly. It seems that another major criterion for establishing the existence of a system would be grammaticality, that is, the existence of a system would imply that sentences which do not conform to the system could occur—ungrammatical contact signing sentences. To determine whether ungrammatical sentences can occur would require grammaticality judgments and such determination is beyond the scope of this study.

Notwithstanding the existence of a system, it would seem that the linguistic background of the individual plays a major role in determining which of those features will show up in the contact signing of that individual. As we suggested earlier, the contact signing produced by a Deaf native user of ASL will probably be somewhat different from the contact signing produced by someone who, while competent in ASL, learned to sign at a later age or from the contact signing produced by a hearing native English speaker who is also a skilled ASL user. We pointed out earlier that Stokoe (personal communication reported in Lee, 1982) suggested that there might exist a PSEd produced by deaf signers and a PSEh produced by hearing signers. We agree that linguistic background of the user plays a role in the outcome of language contact, but his characterization implied the existence of a variety used by more than one person. And this is the same implication contained in the idea of a *continuum of varieties* between English and ASL, an idea that has found widespread acceptance in the Deaf community (Woodward, 1973a). Again, the use of the word *variety* implies the use of the same features by more than one individual. While we find some features consistently used by all of the informants (hence accounting for the intelligibility), we also find a lot of variation among users in the use of other features. We essentially find a consistent set of both ASL and English features with all of the informants, with more English or ASL features occurring according to the individual. This departs from the traditional notion of the continuum, if that notion includes the concept of varieties used by more than one person.

Furthermore, while we see a range of individual variation in which features will occur, and while we can say that contact signing combines features of English and ASL, it is also defined in part by what does *not* occur. For example, even though some individuals use more ASL features than other individuals, we see very few examples of important ASL nonmanual syntactic markers such as occur with topicalization (with the accompanying word order) and no relative clauses. Likewise, while some informants use more English features than other informants and while we do see some signs for bound English morphemes and some single spoken words, we do not see or hear plural -*s*, third-person singular -*s*, possessive -*s*, past tense -*ed*, or comparative -*er*.

Finally, the details of one's linguistic background may not necessarily be predictors of linguistic behavior. For example, we see informants from deaf families using fewer ASL features in contact signing and informants from hearing families using more ASL features. In fact, three of the four informants of the disagreement clips are from hearing families. Also, who one is interacting with may not necessarily be a predictor. We see contact signing with a lot of ASL features with the hearing interviewer and contact signing with fewer ASL features with the Deaf interviewer. Of the inventory of English features in Table 11, there are none that occur only with the hearing interviewer or only with the Deaf interviewer. Of the ASL features, rhetorical questions and locative verbs occur only with the Deaf interviewer, but all other features occur with both hearing and

Deaf. This suggests that other factors must be at work, including how the immediate social situation is perceived, language attitudes about ASL and English, and so forth.

This concludes our discussion of the linguistic features of contact signing. We will now consider the implications of our findings for language contact in general.

CHAPTER 3

Contact Signing in the Context
of Language Contact Studies

Given our description of contact signing as produced by deaf bilinguals in the American Deaf community, we will now approach the question of "So what?" That is, what implications, if any, does our description have for the study of language contact phenomena in general, be they from spoken language or sign language situations? Do our findings make any contribution to a general statement about language contact phenomena? And due to the involvement of two modalities, are any of our findings unique to the contact between a sign language and a spoken language? For an answer to these questions, we return to the themes of reexamination which we outlined in Chapter 1. We will recall Romaine's (1989) observation that much of the research on bilingualism has been conducted within a structuralist framework, with "the belief that an entity, whether it is a society, language or so forth, can be viewed as a structured self-contained whole, an autonomous entity, which is consistent with itself" (p. 286), and that had the research been undertaken by bilinguals in multilingual situations, the resulting picture might be quite different. As more research on language structure and language contact *is* undertaken by bilinguals in multilingual settings, the natural result is the reexamination of earlier claims and constructs. We find that our description has direct bearing on each one of the themes of reexamination that we defined.

The first theme of reexamination that we defined is the one which concerns being able to define various language contact phenomena by unambiguous criteria—that is, being able to unequivocally say, for example, that a given outcome is an instance of borrowing and not an instance of code switching, or being able to unequivocally assign a base language to a stretch of bilingual discourse (Romaine, 1989). It may be simply a natural extension of the perspective on languages as unified wholes that researchers examining the outcome of contact between two unified wholes have attempted to characterize the outcomes also as unified self-contained events, clearly definable and distinct from each other. However, as Romaine illustrates for spoken languages and as our data would seem to indicate for sign language situations, the reality is quite different. In the first place, we saw that we sometimes had difficulty deciding whether a given sign or sequence of signs represented an instance of code switching or contact signing. And we also discussed the possible difficulty in differentiating between code switching and borrowing in the contact between two sign languages. Indeed, given the nature of sign language structures, we discussed the problems that the criterion of phonological integration presents for discussions of borrowing between sign languages and questioned whether the term *borrowing* was always the most accurate characterization of some contact outcomes. As concerns unequivocally assigning a base language to a stretch of bilingual discourse, it seems that it is hard enough to do when the features of the two languages occur *sequentially* in various combinations. In our contact signing data, where the phonological, morphological, syntactic, lexical, and pragmatic features of two different languages are most often produced *simultaneously*, assigning stretches of discourse to ASL or to English seems like a fruitless exercise and also misses the point. The point *is* a third system which combines elements of both languages and may also have some idiosyncratic features. Our data seem to support reexamining the insistence upon unambiguous criteria for defining the various outcomes of language contact.

Related to the issue of criteria for defining contact phenomena is the subissue of particular terms. We have seen that terms that have been applied to spoken language situations, such as *borrowing*, *bilingual*, and *code mixing*, may require reexamination and qualification if they are to be used for describing sign language contact situations. This reexamination may also prove useful for spoken language studies, and we recall Grosjean's (1991) observation that the bilingual is not simply the sum of two complete or incomplete monolinguals, but rather a unique and specific language user. Our data clearly support that observation.

The second theme of reexamination that we introduced in Chapter 1 concerns the focus in language contact studies not on the languages in question, but on the *user*, "the bilingual individual [being] the ultimate locus of contact" (Romaine, 1989, p. 7). Our data support this theme in two ways. In the first place, we have tried to provide an accurate picture of the complexity of bilingualism in the American deaf community, complexity due in large part to the wide variety of linguistic backgrounds that individuals bring with them to contact situations. This variety can be accounted for in part by different etiologies of deafness and in part by the history of deaf education and the respective roles of ASL and English in that history. The overall result is that, while we are willing to say that the predictable appearance of certain features of ASL and English in contact situations makes for a minimal grammar of contact signing, the specific linguistic competence of each individual in a specific contact situation plays a central role in what language forms are produced, the result being that the occurrence of many ASL and English features *cannot* be predicted. As we pointed our earlier, we speculate that what a Deaf native ASL user produces in a contact situation will be different from what a hearing bilingual native English speaker produces. They may both use English word order, signs for English prepositions and conjunctions, English mouthing, and ASL lexical forms, but the Deaf native ASL user may use many more inflected ASL verbs, ASL nonmanual signals, and the establishment of topics in the signing space, while the native English speaker may exploit his knowledge of English collocations, for example. Likewise, a Deaf native ASL user may produce something that is different from someone who signs ASL competently but became deaf in late childhood. Bilingual competence is not monolithic, and the range of competence is necessarily reflected in the outcomes of language contact. We are reminded here of an observation by Strevens (1982):

> . . . a central problem of linguistic study is how to reconcile a convenient and necessary fiction with a great mass of inconvenient facts. The fiction is the notion of a "language"—English, Chinese, Navajo, Kashmiri. The facts reside in the mass of diversity exhibited in the actual performance of individuals when they use a given language. [p. 23]

Now, we identify etiologies of deafness and the history of deaf education as explanations for the differences between the individuals in our study, but our data lead us to ask a question about studies of language contact in spoken language communities. The question is this: Is it possible that individual linguistic backgrounds which seem to play such a central role in the deaf community also play a central role in accounting for spoken language contact behavior, a much more important role than has been realized so far? That is, characteristics of individual backgrounds are not just something that *we* have to deal with in explaining language contact in the deaf community and that may make the deaf community seem unique. Rather, they may play as central a role in spoken language communities, but have been overlooked. Certainly, the role of individual interaction in accounting for variation within a language has been examined in depth in Milroy's studies of social networks (1980), in contrast to classical variation studies which characterize the variable language usage of entire communities. And Gal (1979) also looked at individual usage patterns in her description of Hungarian–German bilingualism. So it is not that the characteristics of the individual have been completely overlooked. We simply suggest that we don't think that deaf communities are unique in this way and that since individual linguistic backgrounds play such a central role in understanding language contact in the deaf community, it stands to reason that they may play an equally important but as yet underestimated role in spoken language contact.

The second way in which our data relate to the theme of focus on the user and not on the language concerns the results of the judgment task which we used to select videotape clips for analysis. We will recall Romaine's (1989) observation that "the recognition of a linguistic system as an autonomous language is ultimately a sociopolitical matter" (p. 283). We see evidence to confirm this observation in two parts of our study: the overall judgment task and the pilot study we conducted. As concerns the overall judgment task, it will be recalled that we found a wide variety of judgments of the clips and very little agreement among the judges. We also suggested that significant disagreement in four of the clips could be accounted for by salient features of ASL that did not occur in the other clips. There may be something else at work, however. While no one will question that there exists a linguistic system known as ASL that is a full-fledged system, isolable and independent from the full-fledged system known as English, it may be that in an intense contact situation such as the one in which our data were collected, the perceived boundaries between the two languages become somewhat fuzzy, and judgments of what is or is not ASL or English may have more to do with sociolinguistic factors such as who is signing, where they are signing, what they are signing about, who is judging, and so forth. In fact, we saw in our pilot study that what the judge was told about the signer seemed to influence the judgment. In addition, there may be some specific linguistic features which may be judged to be part of one or the other language for sociopolitical reasons. Fingerspelling is a good case in point. We feel that we have made the case that while fingerspelling certainly represents the relationship between a sign language phonology and the writing system for a spoken language—that is, that the spoken language has a role—fingerspelling itself is phonologically and morphologically part of the sign language. However, for many years in the American Deaf community, fingerspelling was considered to be English and there was (and still is) active resistance to the idea that fingerspelling is part of the linguistic system of ASL, both among laymen and researchers.[12] Battison (1978), for example, in his pioneering study of fingerspelling as a kind of lexical borrowing, states that

12. Although it is very interesting to note that Stokoe, Casterline, and Cronberg, writers of the first ASL dictionary, observed in 1965 that "it is possible to characterize the manual spelling of English morphemes as a subsystem of ASL. Even though deaf persons may at will use the manual alphabet alone for an exchange and so be using written English as their language, the occurrence of finger spelled [sic] words in a stretch of ASL does not make all signing a subsystem of English. Overwhelming evidence of the opposite view, that manual spelling may be a subsystem within ASL, are the numerous signers who use finger spelled [sic] English words but have little or no control of the syntactical system of English" (p. 291).

"Fingerspelled words . . . are physically and linguistically different from signs in ASL" (p. 218). We suggest that this resistance is due not only to the fact that fingerspelling represents a relationship with English orthography, but also because, as a representation of English, it stood as a symbol of the insistence on English in the educational system and of the suppression and oppression of ASL. Indeed, one educational approach, the Rochester Method, relied on fingerspelling, along with written and spoken English, for the teaching of academic content, to the exclusion of ASL. In informal conversations following the judgment task, some judges suggested that some clips were not ASL because of the presence of fingerspelling, and such judgments have precisely to do with sociopolitical factors, such as the history of language use in deaf education, and not linguistic factors. Another example comes from word order. It appears that ASL and English share the same basic word order in deep structure, SVO (Liddell, 1980). However, for many years there has been resistance to the idea that ASL is an SVO language, in part because to say that would mean that it shared a basic structure with English and this would be politically unacceptable, for the same reasons that fingerspelling was not considered part of ASL. Word order in ASL has been variously described as flexible and not of importance and basically different from word order in English (Fischer, 1975; Friedman, 1976). The basic point here is that, as in spoken language communities, the determination of the status of a given variety in the American Deaf community may sometimes have to do with sociopolitical factors as opposed to linguistic ones.

The third theme of reexamination concerns attempts by researchers to effect a clean separation between individual bilingualism and societal bilingualism. Earlier, we gave Romaine's example of interference, and we will recall her observation that what is seen as interference in an individual's language use may become a norm in community use and that describing interference implies being able to assign a base language to particular stretches of discourse. Our data would seem to indicate that, given the variety of individual linguistic backgrounds, the difficulty in assigning a particular discourse stretch to ASL or English, and the existence, therefore, of a third system, it is hard to isolate instances of "interference" from English or ASL as different from instances of borrowing or code switching. Furthermore, the predictable occurrence of a limited set of contact signing features suggests that what might have been considered interference has evolved into a kind of norm for signing in some contact situations.

Related to both the second and the third themes is the fourth, which has to do with a view of bilingual and contact situations as dynamic as opposed to static. As Romaine (1989) states, "Linguists who study language contact often seek to describe changes at the level of linguistic systems in isolation and abstraction from speakers. Sometimes they tend to treat the outcome of bilingual interaction in static rather than dynamic terms . . ." (p. 7). Our project provides ample evidence for the need for a dynamic perspective. The best example comes from the patterns of overall language use during the interviews, which reveal very rapid and subtle shifting according to interlocutor. The linguistic forms that we ended up describing as "the outcome of language contact" simply cannot be described in isolation and abstraction from the bilingual human beings who produced them. An understanding of the forms hinges upon an understanding of the dynamic social situation in which they occurred. It is dynamic because it changed: We observed signers in five different situations, with different interlocutors, and the signing often changed rapidly and dramatically according to interlocutor characteristics. It is also dynamic because of the variety of linguistic backgrounds that the informants brought with them to the interview situation. While there are certain predictable features of both ASL and English that will appear in contact situations, the linguistic outcome is also highly dynamic because of the variety of linguistic backgrounds of the individuals.

In sum, our project reinforces and provides evidence for the themes of reexamination that emerge from current literature on language contact. By reinforcing the themes of reexamination, our project challenges the traditional perspectives on language contact and bilingualism that have resulted from spoken language studies. Naturally, the question arises as to whether there are any consequences of language contact that have to do specifically with sign languages. We suggest that the answer is both "yes" and "no."

The "yes" has to do with what appear to be some very fundamental differences between spoken language structures and sign language structures, as we described in Chapter 1. We pointed out, for example, that the simply greater number of component parts in sign language phonologies and the greater number of shared component parts *between* sign language phonologies may have consequences for the description of contact phenomena, such as borrowing between sign languages, and what the role of such criteria as phonological integration will turn out to be. As of this writing, research on contact between sign languages is just beginning, and it will be very interesting to see what future investigations reveal. Fundamental differences between sign language morphologies and spoken language morphologies may have the same consequences. For example, in very general terms, while spoken language morphologies make extensive use of affixation of various kinds for inflection and derivation—that is, "adding on" whole units of meaning to create new units of meaning—sign language morphologies seem not to use affixation as extensively; rather, they seem to rearrange portions of the segmental structure of signs to create new meanings. Finally, fundamental differences between sign language syntax and spoken language syntax, particularly the extensive grammatical use of nonmanual signals, may have interesting consequences for contact between sign languages.

The "no" has to do with what human beings, any human beings, do in situations of language contact. A question about language contact in the American Deaf community might be "Why do human beings in that situation use elements from both languages and both modalities?" The simple answer is "Because they can." We suggest that human beings in language contact situations will exploit whatever linguistic resources are available to them to the fullest, and given availability of and competence in two modalities, they will use two modalities. So, in some ways, there is nothing unique about language contact in the deaf community. It is simply another instance of human beings going about the business of exploiting the linguistic resources available to them, resources which happen to include two modalities, for obvious physiological reasons. There *are* two unique things about it, however. First, given two modalities, how they will be used cannot necessarily be predicted. Deaf people may mouth to other deaf people and not use their hands at all; hearing bilinguals may sign to each other when there are no Deaf people present; a Deaf person may speak to a hearing person and the hearing person may answer in ASL with no voice; a Deaf person and a hearing person may produce contact signing with each other, and so forth. Second, there may be some structurally unique outcomes both between two sign languages (many of which have yet to be described) and between a sign language and a spoken language—fingerspelling, mouthing, code switching between a natural sign language and an invented code for the spoken language, CODA-speak, and contact signing—outcomes which we have tried to describe here.

It will be recalled that our original goal was to look at the linguistic outcome of deaf–hearing interaction and to reexamine claims that this outcome is a pidgin. As can be seen from this volume, our investigation took us a long way from our starting point and revealed goals that we didn't even know we had when we started out—for example, considering language contact in the Deaf community in the terms defined for spoken language situations, looking at the broad picture of language contact in the Deaf community, distinguishing between contact between two sign languages and contact between a sign language and a spoken language, and defining a model for the various outcomes of language contact. Most important, our investigation made it very clear to us just how intricate and complex language contact in the American Deaf community is, and that there is plenty of research still to be done on that intricacy and complexity.

Postscript: Implications for
Second Language Learning
and Teaching, Interpreting,
and Deaf Education

We have described our project on one of the outcomes of language contact in the American Deaf community. It seems important to devote a few pages to the possible implications of our study for second-language teaching, for interpreting, and for deaf education. We focus on these three areas for one main reason: each of these areas involves the teaching and learning of language. Given that contact between ASL and English will naturally occur in the American Deaf community and given what we have found about the outcomes of language contact, it seems important to briefly consider the project findings in terms of language teaching and language learning options.

For example, as concerns second-language learning and teaching, we suggest that the input for second-language learners of a sign language may sometimes be contact signing. We are talking here about the learning that takes place in informal conversational settings and not necessarily in formal classroom settings. We make this suggestion because our data show that 21 out of 26 informants used contact signing with the hearing interviewers and two used Signed English. Only two of the white informants and one of the black informants used ASL with the hearing interviewers. There would appear to be a strong tendency to use something other than ASL with hearing people and we suggest that tendency may be even stronger if the deaf person knows that the hearing person is in the process of learning to sign.

As we observed earlier, we are reluctant to call contact signing a variety of ASL or of English. There is a set of predictable linguistic features that do constitute a system, but there also seems to be a great deal of individual variation due to differences in linguistic background. This means that the contact signing input that second-language learners are exposed to may also be highly variable. Furthermore, because most deaf interlocutors are bilingual and manage to make at least some sense out of second-language learner output, deaf interlocutors may not engage in correction of that output. Hence, second-language learner output may also be highly variable contact signing.

Now, these three observations relate to second-language learning primarily in an informal conversation setting. However, several researchers in the area of spoken second-language learning have pointed out the importance of the context of learning in the learning process. Specifically, Brown (1987) suggests that the context of learning may be the source of errors and defines the context as "the classroom with its teacher and materials in the case of school learning, or the social situation in the case of untutored second language learning" (p. 179). Richards (1974) suggests that the teacher or the textbook can lead the learner to make faulty hypotheses about language structure because of a misleading explanation from the teacher, a faulty presentation in the textbook, or because a pattern is rotely memorized but not contextualized. Similarly, Selinker (1972) provides the example of native Serbo–Croatian users who experience difficulty with the he/she distinction in English because the textbooks and materials are all limited to the use of *he*. Another example comes from the experience of both authors of this volume in teaching spoken Italian and ASL respectively, to adults. As a near-native user of Italian, one author's instincts are that *formal* pronouns are most appropriate in social interaction with unfamiliar adults, and she has to make a conscious effort to teach and use the informal forms in class so that her students have full exposure to the complete system. As a near-native user of ASL, the other author reports that before teaching an ASL class, he must remind himself that he must use ASL in that situation, as a situation with all hearing English-speaking participants tends to induce the production of contact signing. Stenson (1974) introduces the concept of "induced errors" in second-language learning, and Corder (1971) refers to the idiosyncratic dialects that may result from second-language learning in formal classroom contexts. The point here is simply that the social context in which a language is being learned may *itself* play a key role in the learning process, and it may help determine what is learned (Gaies, 1977).

Our fourth observation, then, is that the concept of the context of learning would seem to have a great deal of relevance for the teaching and learning of sign languages as well as spoken languages. If, as our data indicate, Deaf native signers of ASL very often do not produce ASL in the presence of hearing people in ordinary conversational settings, what does this mean for the formal instruction of ASL as a second language to hearing people? For the instruction of ASL as a second language, the context of learning closely reflects one of the ordinary social situations in which deaf people do not use ASL, that is, with hearing people. Is the fact that the situation is a formal second-language learning setting enough to guarantee that ASL will be produced, even though the interlocutors are hearing non-native signers? In fact, there is an abundance of anecdotal evidence from learners that teachers produce contact signing and also of accounts from teachers of the difficulty encountered in producing ASL in a classroom setting, as opposed to producing contact signing. Empirical research on language use in sign language classrooms will be useful. Furthermore, given the range of language use that we have observed, it seems that instruction in ASL will provide students the most access to whatever they may encounter. If they are taught ASL, they will be able to understand contact signing, which will sometimes naturally occur. On the other hand, if they are taught contact signing, they will probably not be able to understand ASL. The issue is one of language use versus language instruction: The fact that contact signing will naturally occur does not justify teaching it formally, because it cannot provide access to the full range of language use that a student will see. ASL can provide that access and would seem to be the most appropriate target language for second-language learners.

To ensure that ASL is being taught (as opposed to contact signing), the training of Deaf adults as sign language instructors should perhaps include overt exposure to a realistic picture of language use in the Deaf community in all its complexity. Specifically, teacher training might include the identification on videotapes of different kinds of signing and a discussion of what accounts for the differences; the keeping of a record by prospective teachers of their own sign use in different social situations, along with some note about the linguistic features that distinguish different kinds of signing; formal exposure to the linguistic structure of ASL through a basic linguistics course; and analysis and critique of videotapes of actual teaching sessions, taught by prospective teachers. An awareness of the structural differences between ASL and contact signing and an awareness of their own use of sign language in different settings might be useful to teachers. To our knowledge, while a number of methodologies have been proposed and developed for the teaching of sign language, there is no discussion in the literature, to date, of the need for conscious sociolinguistic awareness as part of teacher training, nor is there any discussion of the role of the context of learning in the teaching of sign language. (See, for example, Caccamise and Hicks, 1978; Caccamise, Garretson, and Bellugi, 1982; Lentz, Mikos, and Smith, 1988.)

We speak here of the American Deaf community and of the relationship between ASL and contact signing. It seems, however, that a realistic picture of language use and a realistic look at the kind of signing that Deaf native users produce with hearing nonnative users in ordinary conversational settings might be of relevance to any Deaf community in which sign language instruction is being implemented. Indeed, a realistic representation of language use in a Deaf community may be the first step in the development of an instructional program.

As far as interpreting is concerned, an issue that is consistently addressed in texts, handbooks, and workshop materials on sign language interpreting is the issue of language assessment. That is, as a part of their preparation for an interpreting assignment, sign language interpreters are advised to do an assessment of the com-

munication characteristics of a given situation. These characteristics include the communication skills and communication pref-
erence of the consumers and the social nature and the setting of the
interaction. The goal of the assessment is for the interpreter to be
able to adequately accommodate the clients' communication preferences, thereby providing the most appropriate interpreting possible. For example, Caccamise *et al.* (1980) devoted a section of
their manual on interpreting to the importance of communication
and language preferences and skills of consumers, and they provide
guidelines on conducting assessment. Neumann Solow (1981)
states that the skill of interpreters rests in part on their ability to
make the appropriate decisions regarding communication choices,
and Witter-Merithew (1982) includes the language assessment as
one of the five general phases of assessment associated with each
interpreting assignment (the other four being preassignment, environment, self, and postassignment). One objective for a legal interpreting workshop offered in Little Rock, Arkansas, states that
"Given a variety of role-play situations with deaf persons of ranging
communication styles, participants will be able to select the appropriate language or communication mode and interpret with 80%
accuracy" (Taff-Watson and Duncan, 1987, p. 64; see also Northrup
and Taff-Watson, 1987, and Taff-Watson and Northrup, 1988). Finally, in her textbook on interpreting, Frishberg (1986) observes
that interpreters

> must also have excellent sign language skills, including a range of variation
> from American Sign Language through a multitude of ways of incorporat-
> ing English into a visual–gestural code. . . . They must be flexible in their
> own usage in order to accommodate clients from differing age groups,
> ethnic origins, social and educational backgrounds. . . . In both language
> modes (spoken and signed), the interpreter needs to be able to match any
> speaker encountered for register. . . . The interpreter must adapt to circum-
> stances. [p. 26]

It is clear that effective assessment is based upon a recognition of
diversity in ways of communicating in the American Deaf community and upon an awareness that, because of the diversity, there
may exist more than one language choice in a given interpreting
situation. This is due to the wide variety of linguistic and educational backgrounds that interpreters and deaf clients bring to inter-

preting situations, a variety that we have described earlier in this volume. In fact, all of the sources that we consulted use the labels commonly assigned to different ways of communicating, that is, ASL, MCE (Manually Coded English), and PSE (Pidgin Sign English), and most of the sources stress the need for interpreters to be able to differentiate the specific features of the different modes. This need would seem to presume linguistic descriptions of the different modes upon which interpreter educators and interpreters could base their assessments.

In this volume, we have presented a linguistic and sociolinguistic description of language contact in the American Deaf community. Language use in the American Deaf community is complex and diverse; it is by no means simple or uniform. As our data demonstrate, there are a number of reasons—formality, lack of familiarity, the topic at hand, a desire to demonstrate solidarity—that Deaf people may not use ASL with each other or may choose to use ASL with hearing people. We have suggested that the occurrence of contact signing among deaf people (when no hearing people are present) is probably a reflection of the educational and social reality in which ASL has been devalued and that the situation may change as ASL becomes more accepted by Deaf people in all social situations. However, at this point, the fact remains that Deaf people don't always use ASL with each other, and this may be reflected in requests for interpreting. A Deaf person may not see ASL as the only appropriate choice for an interpreting situation, and he or she may regard forms that are other than ASL as appropriate. Furthermore, as our data reveal, different modes may occur simultaneously in one setting, rendering assessment difficult. Simply, an interpreter who is taught to match a consumer may observe correctly that consumers don't match *each other*. Finally, we observed that most of our informants did use contact signing with hearing interviewers, and an interpreter could similarly find his or her status as an interpreter competing with his or her status as a hearing person. That is, the client might not sign ASL with an interpreter by virtue of the fact that he or she is hearing.

Consider, for example, the differences in language skills and educational backgrounds of four different individuals who might find themselves in an interpreting situation: (1) an individual from a Deaf family who was born hearing and became deaf as an adolescent and has native competence in both ASL and English, (2) an individual who was born to hearing parents and really had no exposure to a linguistic system until age 3 upon arrival at the residential school and who has native competence in ASL and second-language competence in English, (3) an individual born deaf to Deaf parents who learned ASL natively and, by virtue of having a language base established at an early age, has near-native competence in English, and (4) a hearing person who is a native English speaker and a second-language user of ASL. The relative command of both ASL and English will clearly be different for each individual and will clearly play a role in an interpreting situation. Specifically, we see it having a role in situations in which the Deaf person chooses to sign and the interpreter's task is to interpret into spoken English. For the variety of sociolinguistic factors that we have discussed, what the interpreter sees may be contact signing, a third system which combines elements of both ASL and English in varying proportions.

The issue for interpreting is the same as for second-language learning: What is the best way to provide interpreters access to the complexity and diversity of language use in the American Deaf community, access they need both for assessing the situation and for interpreting? It seems that bilingualism in ASL and English will provide access to the full range. While interpreters may see contact signing, learning only contact signing will not allow them to understand or produce ASL if needed.

Finally, we have seen that contact between ASL and English is closely tied to the history of deaf education in the United States. Not that language contact is restricted to educational settings, but the history of deaf education has played a central role in determining the outcome of language contact, with its overwhelming emphasis on the instruction of English, with the explicit exclusion of ASL as a medium of instruction, with the variety of instructional methods that have been tried resulting in children and adults with a wide variety of linguistic backgrounds. There would be contact between English and ASL in the American Deaf community even if the medium of instruction had always been ASL from the very inception of deaf education, because of the respective functions of ASL and English in the lives of deaf people who are at once members of the deaf community and members of American society at large. And this contact would result in linguistic outcomes. Now, since the focus in deaf education has been explicitly on the instruction of

English, including spoken English, and on the use of manual codes for English as the medium of instruction, the contact between the two languages has been unique and its outcomes may be somewhat different than a bilingual situation in which two languages are simply recognized as having equal status as viable linguistic systems and separate functions. We should recall that the contact between the hearing users of a spoken language and the deaf users of a sign language may not always have the outcomes that we see in the United States, particularly in situations such as the Yucatan community in which all community members sign.

So, the contact between ASL and English in the American Deaf community has some of the characteristics of any language contact situation and linguistic outcomes can be expected from that contact as they can be expected from any situation in which two languages are in contact; it has some unique characteristics resulting from the particular sociolinguistic relationship between ASL and English and from the use of two modalities.

Once again, as with second-language learning and interpreting, the issue is how best to provide students access to the full range of language use in the American Deaf community, access which seems desirable for full participation in the community. And once again, it seems that using ASL will provide the best access. Teachers need to understand their students and students need to understand their teachers. Parents and children want to understand each other. Once again, there is a difference between language use and language instruction. Contact signing will naturally occur in educational settings, but its occurrence does not seem to justify its use as the medium of instruction or its being taught to parents, to prospective teachers, and to students, because contact signing alone cannot provide access to the full range of language use that parents, teachers, and students will see. In fact, this observation has been incorporated into the bilingual programs implemented in Sweden, in which the focus is explicitly on Swedish Sign Language and written Swedish, to the exclusion of the signing that results from the contact between Swedish Sign Language and spoken Swedish (Davies, 1991). It would seem, then, that in addition to providing some insight on the nature of language use in the American Deaf community, our findings may also have some implications for the everyday lives of the people in that community.

Raw Percentages of
Judgment Task

Clip #	1	2	3	4	5	6	7	8
Master	ASL W	NA W	NA W	NA B	NA W	NA B	NA W	NA W
Linguists(n=11) 1st judgment	$\frac{11}{11}$	$\frac{11}{11}$	$\frac{9}{11}$	$\frac{4}{11}$	$\frac{5}{11}$	$\frac{10}{11}$	$\frac{9}{11}$	$\frac{8}{11}$
	100	100	81	36	45	90	81	72
2nd judgment	$\frac{11}{11}$	$\frac{11}{11}$	$\frac{9}{11}$	$\frac{3}{11}$	$\frac{6}{11}$	$\frac{11}{11}$	$\frac{9}{11}$	$\frac{10}{11}$
	100	100	81	27	54	100	81	90
Black Community (n=8) 1st judgment	$\frac{7}{8}$	$\frac{6}{8}$	$\frac{5}{8}$	$\frac{5}{8}$	$\frac{3}{8}$	$\frac{5}{8}$	$\frac{2}{8}$	$\frac{5}{8}$
	87	75	62	62	37	62	25	62
2nd judgment	$\frac{6}{8}$	$\frac{6}{8}$	$\frac{3}{8}$	$\frac{3}{8}$	$\frac{2}{8}$	$\frac{5}{8}$	$\frac{5}{8}$	$\frac{7}{8}$
	75	75	37	37	25	62	62	87
White Community (n=11) 1st judgment	$\frac{11}{11}$	$\frac{11}{11}$	$\frac{11}{11}$	$\frac{1}{11}$	$\frac{3}{11}$	$\frac{10}{11}$	$\frac{4}{11}$	$\frac{6}{11}$
	100	100	100	9	27	90	36	54
2nd judgment	$\frac{11}{11}$	$\frac{10}{11}$	$\frac{11}{11}$	$\frac{2}{11}$	$\frac{5}{11}$	$\frac{10}{11}$	$\frac{4}{11}$	$\frac{8}{11}$
	100	100	100	18	45	90	36	72
All (n=30) 1st judgment	$\frac{29}{30}$	$\frac{28}{30}$	$\frac{25}{30}$	$\frac{10}{30}$	$\frac{11}{30}$	$\frac{25}{30}$	$\frac{15}{30}$	$\frac{19}{30}$
	96	93	83	33	36	83	50	63
2nd judgment	$\frac{28}{30}$	$\frac{27}{30}$	$\frac{23}{30}$	$\frac{8}{30}$	$\frac{13}{30}$	$\frac{26}{30}$	$\frac{18}{30}$	$\frac{25}{30}$
	93	90	76	26	43	86	60	83

9	10	11	12	13	14	15	16	17	18	19	20
NA W	ASL B	NA B	ASL W	NA B	NA B	NA W	NA B	ASL W	ASL B	NA W	NA B
$\frac{11}{11}$	$\frac{10}{11}$	$\frac{7}{11}$	$\frac{10}{11}$	$\frac{6}{11}$	$\frac{11}{11}$	$\frac{10}{11}$	$\frac{2}{11}$	$\frac{11}{11}$	$\frac{10}{11}$	$\frac{11}{11}$	$\frac{8}{11}$
100	90	63	90	54	100	90	18	100	90	100	72
$\frac{11}{11}$	$\frac{10}{11}$	$\frac{6}{11}$	$\frac{9}{11}$	$\frac{8}{11}$	$\frac{11}{11}$	$\frac{10}{11}$	$\frac{2}{11}$	$\frac{11}{11}$	$\frac{8}{11}$	$\frac{11}{11}$	$\frac{10}{11}$
100	90	54	81	72	100	90	18	100	72	100	90
$\frac{6}{8}$	$\frac{7}{8}$	$\frac{4}{8}$	$\frac{4}{8}$	$\frac{3}{8}$	$\frac{1}{8}$	$\frac{3}{8}$	$\frac{0}{8}$	$\frac{6}{8}$	$\frac{6}{8}$	$\frac{2}{8}$	$\frac{2}{8}$
75	87	50	50	37	12	37	0	75	75	25	25
$\frac{5}{8}$	$\frac{7}{8}$	$\frac{3}{8}$	$\frac{5}{8}$	$\frac{3}{8}$	$\frac{2}{8}$	$\frac{4}{8}$	$\frac{0}{8}$	$\frac{6}{8}$	$\frac{7}{8}$	$\frac{4}{8}$	$\frac{1}{8}$
62	87	37	62	37	25	50	0	75	87	50	12
$\frac{10}{11}$	$\frac{10}{11}$	$\frac{6}{11}$	$\frac{9}{11}$	$\frac{8}{11}$	$\frac{8}{11}$	$\frac{7}{11}$	$\frac{1}{11}$	$\frac{10}{11}$	$\frac{8}{11}$	$\frac{10}{11}$	$\frac{9}{11}$
90	90	54	81	72	72	63	9	90	72	90	81
$\frac{11}{11}$	$\frac{10}{11}$	$\frac{2}{11}$	$\frac{9}{11}$	$\frac{6}{11}$	$\frac{6}{11}$	$\frac{7}{11}$	$\frac{1}{11}$	$\frac{11}{11}$	$\frac{10}{11}$	$\frac{6}{11}$	$\frac{9}{11}$
100	90	18	81	54	54	63	9	100	90	54	81
$\frac{26}{30}$	$\frac{27}{30}$	$\frac{17}{30}$	$\frac{23}{30}$	$\frac{17}{30}$	$\frac{20}{30}$	$\frac{20}{30}$	$\frac{3}{30}$	$\frac{26}{30}$	$\frac{24}{30}$	$\frac{23}{30}$	$\frac{19}{30}$
86	90	56	76	56	66	66	10	86	80	76	63
$\frac{27}{30}$	$\frac{27}{30}$	$\frac{11}{30}$	$\frac{23}{30}$	$\frac{17}{30}$	$\frac{19}{30}$	$\frac{21}{30}$	$\frac{3}{30}$	$\frac{27}{30}$	$\frac{25}{30}$	$\frac{21}{30}$	$\frac{20}{30}$
90	90	36	76	56	63	70	10	90	83	70	66

Transcriptions of
Videotaped Segments

SEGMENT #2

                                        +M ————————————————————▶
         neg   neg
_____
PRO:1   AGREE   PRO: 1   AGREE   THAT   BECAUSE   PRO:1

                                                        ————————————▶
         brow up   gaze cntr
_____
SUPPORT   DEAF   INSTITUTION   BECAUSE   PRO: 3-center

+M ——▶
gaze cntr   gaze cntr   gaze cntr
_____
MORE   ATTENTION   ON   SPECIFIC   #OF   LIFE   #STYLE   AND

         +M ——▶
              gaze cntr   gaze cntr
_____
PRO:3-center MORE GENERAL GOOD #ED DEPEND ON WHAT STATE

_____
                                                                    ▶
_____
WHICH PLACE HAVE BEST DEPEND ON PEOPLE'S EXPERIENCE

         +M ———————————————————————————— "so" ————————————————▶
                                                        gaze cntr
_____
"WELL" BACKGROUND #OF TEACH ING COOPERATIVE TEAM

_____
                                          ——————————————▶
              gaze cntr   nodding
_____
WORK   #IS   REAL   MOST   KEY   THEIR   #GOALS   ETC   #OK

I don't agree with that because I support deaf residential schools because they place more
attention on the specifics of lifestyle, and the education, in general, is better—depending on
what state, which place has the best—that depends on the people's experience, on their
teaching background—so, cooperative teamwork is really the key to their goals.

SEGMENT #3

+M ——▶
gaze down (looking at paper) ···▶

PRO:1 THINK WILL FIRST PRO.1 AGREE THAT A GALLAUDET

————————————————————————————▶   +M ——————————————▶
···▶

PRESIDENT SHOULD #BE DEAF NOT *REQUIRE* #REQUIREMENT ON

+M ————————————————————▶   rhet ——————————————————▶
        gaze cntr   gaze cntr

#JOB #DESCRIPTION (2h) 1-CL'rectangle' SAY WORDS-WRITTEN

————————————————————————————————————▶

REQUIRE DEAF SKILL USE-ASL THAT'S-NOT-WHAT-I'M-SAYING

+M ————————————————————————————————▶
        gaze down ·······································▶

BUT HAVE A PERSON WHO QUALIFY ENOUGH HAPPEN DEAF FINE

+M ———

AND WILL GIVE MORE MEAN TO GALLAUDET PRO:1 THINK BECAUSE

"they" ——

PRO:3 MANY OF STUDENT ARE DEAF #IS A LA (Liberal Arts) COLLEGE

——
                    gaze up lf ·······························▶

FOR DEAF HAVE A DEAF PRESIDENT ALSO ROLE #MODEL WHEN

——————————————————————————————————▶

MAKE POINT WORTH#WHILE "WELL"

I think—I'll answer first—I agree that a Gallaudet president should be deaf—not that it should be on-the-job description, with words that say it requires a deaf person skilled in the use of ASL—that's not what I'm saying. But if there's a person who's qualified enough who happens to be deaf, fine, and it will give more meaning to Gallaudet. I think that because many of the students are deaf and it's a liberal arts college for the deaf. To have a deaf president and also a deaf role model, when he makes a point, it will be worthwhile.

SEGMENT #6

+M

gaze down · ➤

PRO:1 DISAGREE BECAUSE IT MAKE ME FEEL LIKE PRO:1 CAN'T

➤   +M

              gaze down · ➤

#DO ANYTHING FOR MYSELF "WELL" FEEL "UMM" #THEY #TREAT

➤   +M

     gaze down · ➤

ME DIFFERENT "WELL" WHEN PRO.1 KNOW THAT PRO:1 CAN #DO

· · · · · · · · · · · · · · ➤   *gaze cntr*   *gaze cntr*

SOMETHING LET ME TRY AND (2h)GIVE-me ME TIME TO ASK

        gaze cntr   *taking role of PRO:3*

PRO:3-center FOR HELP, NOT JUST MEET-me AND /"OH" SORRY /

➤

gaze cntr   *(head shaking)*

FEEL LIKE PRO:3 cntr SORRY FOR ME YOU-KNOW

I disagree because it makes me feel like I can't do anything for myself—well, I feel, um, like they treat me differently when I know that I can do something—let me try and give me time to ask them for help, instead of just meeting me and acting like they feel sorry for me, you know.

SEGMENT #7

```
          +M ──────────────────────────────────────────►
    gaze down
```
PRO:1 FEEL... YES TRUE HAVE COMMUNICATION PROBLEMS YES

```
+M ──────────►   +M ──────────────────►
                                        gaze down ········
```
INTERPRETER YES SOMETIMES PAINFUL AND-SO-FORTH BUT PRO.1

```
+M ──────────────────────►   +M ──────────────►
·····················►                gaze up
```
FEEL DEAF PERSON DET-lf HAVE RIGHT (correct herself)

```
+M ────────────────────────────────►        +M ──
                "accurate"
```
POSITIVE PERSONALITY RIGHT PERSONALITY LIKE-THAT CAN

```
────────────────────►   +M ──────────────────────
        gaze down                        gaze down ···
```
INFLUENCE HEARING PERSON PRO.1 FROM MY EXPERIENCE PRO.1

```
────────────────────────►   +M ── "even though" ──────
·····························►
```
KNOW-THAT SOME DEAF PEOPLE DET-lf DOESN'T-MATTER THROUGH

```
──────────►   +M ──────────────►
                            gaze down ··
```
INTERPRETER WOW REALLY MAKE IMP- BIG IMPACT INFLUENCE DEAF

```
        +M ──────────────────►
·······························►
```
(correct herself) HEARING PEOPLE

I feel . . . yes, true, there are communication problems and yes, sometimes it's painful with the interpreter and so forth, but I feel that if the deaf person has the right . . . a positive personality, they can influence the hearing person. I know from my experience that some deaf people really make a big impact on deaf . . . I mean hearing people, even if they're using an interpreter.

SEGMENT #8

+M ———————————————————————————————▶

#THEY HAVE I-N-K-L-I-N-G #OF WHAT DEAF CULTURE #IS ABOUT

+M ——————————————▶ +M ——————————▶
gaze up

"WELL" EXPOSURE TO #IT (2h)SEE-alt "WELL" NOT IDIOT,

+M ————————▶ +M ——— "able" ——————————————▶
gaze rt   *gaze rt*   *gaze down*

"WELL" NOT BEHIND "WELL" NOT CAN TO COMMUNICATE SIGN

+M ——— "I am" ————— "ing" ——————▶ +M ——————▶
gaze down ···

"WELL" NOT SAY THAT INDEX ARE "WELL" #BONAFIDE

—————————————▶ +M ——▶
···

MEMBER OF DEAF CULTURE 100% SUPPORT AGREE NO BUT "WELL"

+M ————————————————————▶
gaze lf ······················· *gaze lf, up* ·····················

PRO.1 SURE HEAR MANY TIME DEAF USE-ASL-TO FIND HEARING

················▶ *gaze back to right* ·································

PARENTS DEAF OH-I-SEE NO-WONDER INDEX-lf PRO.1 DON'T-KNOW

······················▶

PRO:3-left "WELL".

They have an inkling of what deaf culture is about, exposure to it; they've seen it repeatedly. They're not idiots, they're not behind, not . . . they can communicate in sign. I'm not saying they're bonafide members of deaf culture—I don't agree with that 100%, no, but I'm sure that many times a deaf person using ASL will find out that the other person is hearing with deaf parents and will say "Oh, now I see . . . no wonder . . . I didn't know that."

SEGMENT #14

+M ——————————————————————— "I" ———————————
gaze down, brow up ···►

RIGHT NOW PRO:1 SEE MYSELF   (2h) HAVE SOME WHITES BEGIN

——————————————►
gaze down

SOCIALIZE A-JUST-LITTLE-BIT, NOT ALL, A-LITTLE-BIT "WELL"

+M ———————————————————————►   +M ———————————————
gaze down   gaze down

TIME NOT ALWAYS CHANGE THAT FAST "WELL" IN WAY #SPORTS

+M ———————————————►   +M ——— "they" ———————————
gaze cntr

#IF INVOLVE DEPEND SOCIALIZE-WITH   DON'T WHAT PRO.1

——————————— "that is" ———————————————————►

THINK BECAUSE WHY WE WON'T BITE PRO:2 "WELL"

Right now, I see for myself that some whites have begun to socialize just a little bit, not all of them, a little bit—times don't always change that fast—in a way, sports . . . if one is involved, it depends on who you socialize with—but they don't—what I think, it's because we won't bite you.

SEGMENT #15

```
+M ─────────────────────────────────────────────────────────────
```
PRO:1 SAY THAT QUESTION NOT BROUGHT UP IN FIRST PLACE

```
─────────────────────────────────────────────── "of" ─────
                                    neg        gaze down
```
PRO:1 DISAGREE BECAUSE WE SHOULD NOT DISCUSS KIND   QUES-

```
                                          ──────────────────▶
        gaze lf                gaze lf              gaze rt
```
TION BECAUSE CAN # BE ANY ONE DEAF "OR" HEARING DOESN'T-

```
            +M ──────────────────▶
        gaze lf              gaze lf    gaze rt
```
MATTER FEEL LOOK-AT TODAY DEAF HEARING DOESN'T MATTER

```
+M ──────────────────────────────────────────────────────▶
gaze lf · · · · · · · · · · · · · · · · · · · · ·▶
```
QUESTION SAY PRESIDENT #OF GALLAUDET *SHOULD* #BE DEAF

```
            +M ─────────────────────────────────────────▶
  neg          gaze lf
```
PRO:1 AGREE BECAUSE PRO:1 HAVE-TO LOOK ON THAT QUALIFIED

```
            +M ──────────────────────────────▶
        gaze lf          gaze cntr       cond
```
DEAF PERSON DET WANT BECOME PRESIDENT, HAVE LIST-OF-

```
                +M ──────────────────▶
        cond          gaze lf
```
QUALIFICATIONS CAN, FINE BECAUSE. . . .

I say that question isn't brought up in the first place—I disagree because we should not discuss that kind of question because it can be a deaf person or a hearing person, it doesn't matter- I feel, look at today, deaf or hearing, doesn't matter. The question asks if the president of Gallaudet should be deaf—I don't agree because I have to look at that qualified deaf person if he wants to become president—and if he has the list of qualifications, fine, because. . . .

SEGMENT #19

                                        +M ——— "out that we are" ——————————————————————————

BECAUSE INFORM FIND   DEAF HELP US BECAUSE

— "they" ——————————————————————— "to" —————————— "that" ——————————

     SERVE [U]S THEIR PURPOSE   MAKE SURE   THEY MEET

————————————— "because" ————— "of" ————— "have no" ————— "to" ——————————
                                                                      gaze rt

OUR   NEEDS.   MANY   [U]S NONE TIME   WARN++

+M ——————————————————————————▶   +M ———————————————————▶
                                                              cond

WHO RIGHT PERSON TELL "NOT-CLEAR" AGREE FIND DEAF

                +M ————————————————————————————————————
                                      cond   "no"

1-CL'come up' HELP, FINE NOT NEED #IT, TELL-PRO:3. NONE

————————————— "don't" ————————————————— "thank you" ——————▶

THANK-YOU   NEED YOUR HELP BUT INFORM-PRO:3.

Because they're informed, they find out that we are deaf; they help us because they serve us. Their purpose is to make sure that they meet our needs. Because many of us have no time to warn them who the right person is—I agree, if someone finds out you're deaf and comes up and offers help, fine . . . if you don't need it, tell them "No thank you, I don't need your help," but let them know.

SEGMENT #20

+M ────────────────────────────▶
gaze down

PRO:1 FEEL PRO:1 #WOULD TALK ABOUT MYSELF PRO:1 WONDER

+M ──────────────────▶   +M ─────────────
gaze lf

PRO:1 PLAN FAMILY #REUNION (2h)#SO PRO:1 (2h)INVITE-alt #ALL

MY [R]ELATIVES FAMILY COME TO WDC #SO WE HAVE WORK-SHOP

──────▶

ABOUT DEAF CULTURE BECAUSE MY FAMILY DON'T-KNOW ABOUT

+M ────────────────────▶

DEAF CULTURE "WELL" PR O:1 WANT PRO:3 GET THEIR EXPERIENCE

+M ──────▶   +M ────────────────▶

ABOUT DEAF PRO:1 WANT, MY MOTHER *NOT* HAVE ANY EXPERIENCE

+M ──▶
gaze down

THAT WHY PRO:1 ENCOURAGE-them, PRO:1 CONSIDER, THAT WHY

PRO:1   PLAN.

I feel that I would talk about myself . . . I wonder . . . I plan a family reunion so I can invite all of my relatives to come to Washington, D.C., so we can have a workshop about deaf culture because my family doesn't know about deaf culture—I want them to experience about the deaf—I want—my mother doesn't have any experience—that's why I encourage them, I consider, that's why I plan.

SEGMENT #4

+M ————————————————➤   +M ——➤
                gaze lf   *gaze lf*

THINK STRONG AGREE SAME BECAUSE DEPEND ON THEIR PARENTS

             +M ——➤
gaze lf

GROW-UP WHERE SCHOOL INDEX-rt'school' SAY NO DIFFERENT
                     INDEX-lf'other school'

        gaze down ···➤

WHITE I MEAN WHITE AND BLACK DEAF(black) DEAF(white) SAME

+M ————————————————————————————————

UNLESS WHAT INFLUENCE FROM ENVIRONMENT, FROM FAMILY,

————————————————➤

(2h)GROW-UP WHERE. THAT "WELL"

I think that I strongly agree because it depends on their parents, where they grew up, where the school was. I say that there's no difference between white and black, black deaf and white deaf are the same except for influence from the environment, from family, from where you grow up.

SEGMENT #5

+M ────────────────────────────────▶
                 gaze lf   *gaze lf*

NEVER HEARD PARLIAMENTARY, MEETING, #ADJ "I can't understand"

         +M ──────────────────── "regretful" ─────────
    gaze lf

#OUT PRO:1 KEEP-GOING-ON BUT PRO:1 FEEL NOT SORRY THAT

                                   gaze up

PRO:1 GRADUATE FROM MAINSTREAM BUT PRO:1 A-LITTLE-BIT

"regretful" ──

SORRY THAT PRO:1 LOUSY (2h)#ED DEAF (2h)#ED PRO:1

─── "regretful" ───▶   +M ──▶   +M ───
               gaze down

NOT SORRY THAT TOOK+ COURSES KNOW (2h)THEIR-alt BUT

──▶   +M ───
gaze rt

DEAF SELF NOT-SO-HOT #SO THEIR RESIDENTIAL-SCHOOL IN MY

─────────────▶   +M ────────────────────

HOME STATE TEXAS DET FIND THAT RESIDENTIAL-SCHOOL #AUSTIN

──▶   +M ── "social" ─▶   +M ──────

RIGHT PRO:1 INTERACT INDEX-rt "OOPS" PRO:1 MEAN CAMP

         +M ──▶   +M ── "social" ──────
         brow frown ·······································

INTERACT INDEX-rt #OK FOUND THEIR FINEwg SITUATION LIFE

"leadership" ▶   +M ───────────────────▶
·················▶

LEADER ETC BUT FOUND THEIR #ED SO-SO PRO:1 LIKE

(continued)

SEGMENT #5 *continued*

<table>
<tr><td></td><td>neg</td><td>brow up</td></tr>
</table>

"WELL" PRO:1 "LOOK-AT-THAT" BOTH ADVANTAGE THEIR ADVANTAGE

+M ———— "leadership" ——
        neg   brow up

LEADER #ED PRO:1 ADVANTAGE INTERACT WITH HEARING KNOW

⟶

PREPARE IN [F]UTURE "I-DON'T-KNOW" INDEX-lf-alt "WELL"
INDEX-rt-alt

I never heard of parliamentary procedure, meetings, adjectives—that was out. I kept going but I don't feel sorry that I graduated from a mainstream program but I'm a little bit sorry that I had a lousy education—I'm not sorry that I took courses and know the two different ways but deaf education is not so hot. So . . . their residential school in my home state of Texas . . . I find that at that residential school—Austin, right . . . I interacted a lot socially—oops, I mean I interacted a lot at camp, ok, and, found that socially and leadershipwise, it was fine, but the education was so-so—Both have their advantages—mainstreaming is not so good for leadership but it has the advantage of interacting with hearing people and helps prepare for the future.

SEGMENT #11

| | gaze down | | | gaze rt | | gaze lf |

PRO:1 AGREE INDEX-paper SAY #AGE "WELL" BLACK #ED WHITE

+M——" they are" ——————————➤

#ED A-LITTLE-BIT "WELL" PRETTY GOOD   TRUE SAME SOME

+M

| | rhet-q | | t | neg | | t | |

DIFFERENT WHY   BLACK #ED   BLACK PEOPLE LITTLE-BIT WEAK

+M ——

| | | gaze rt | |

HAVE BACKGROUND #ED BECAUSE DEPEND FAMILY [P]ARENTS DON'T

——————————➤   +M ——————➤

UNDERSTAND ABOUT DEAF NESS ETC REAL #LY NONE BUT A-BIT

+M ——————————➤

OTHER DEAF BLACK LUCKY LEARN FROM WHITE #ED DET BUT

| | | | | gaze lf |

"WELL" DEAF PEOPLE LEARN PRO:3(Black) WILL #IF SOCIALIZE-

+M ——————➤

WITH (GROW-UP) WHITE PEOPLE WILL BE #OK

I agree . . . I'd say age . . . well, black education and white education are pretty good . . . they are the same with some differences because black education . . . black people are a little bit weak in having background education because it depends on the family, on parents who don't understand about deafness and so forth . . . really no understanding . . . a bit. Other black deaf are lucky because they learn from white education but, deaf people learn . . . they will learn if they socialize with white people, they'll be OK.

SEGMENT #16

```
+M ——— "s" ————————▶
          brow up              gaze down · · · · · · · · · · · · · · · · · · · · · · · · · · · · · · · · · · · ·▶gaze cntr · · · · · · · · · · · · ·
```
WHAT   MORE THAT PRO:3-rt BLACK, WHITE TEACHER PRO:3-rt WHITE

```
+M ————————————————————————————▶
t · · · · · · · · · · · · · · · · · · · · · · · · · · · · · · · · · · · · · · · · · · · ·▶
```
TEACHER NOT ENOUGH TEACH-lf BLACK PRO:3-lf STUDENT PRO:3-lf

```
                              +M ———▶
        gaze down                              gaze rt · · · · · · · · · · · · · · · · · · · · · · · · · · · · · · · · · · · · ·
```
teacher-TEACH-students ENGLISH ETC. PRO:3-rt MOTIVATED TO TEACH

```
· · · · · · · · · · · · · · · · · · · · ·▶       gaze rt, down· · · · · · · · · · · · · · · · · · taking role of teacher
```
WHITE   CHILDREN   DET/TEACH   EXPLAIN   DEAL-WITH   NOT   LOOK-lf/

```
+M ——————————————————————————▶
              gaze down                    gaze up      taking role of a black student
```
BLACK TRY HARD WITH THAT ENGLISH /CALL-ON-TEACHER INSIST/

```
              gaze down        taking role of teacher        gaze lf
```
PRO:3(teacher) /HOLD-ON, QUICK-EXPLANATION SHORT FINISH SHORT

```
              taking role of teacher                                    rhet
```
/KEEP-DISTANCE GO-BACK-WITH-WHITE-CHILDREN/ WHY SEE PAH

```
+M ———————————————————————————————————
      gaze down
```
T-H-O-M-A-S B-I-R-D ONE PASS BLACK, BLACK T-H-O-M-A-S ONE,

```
gaze rt                              gaze lf
```
ALL WHITE GO GALLAUDET WE BLACK FAIL THAT HOW WHITE

```
————————————————————————————————————▶
```
TEACHERS NOT ENOUGH TEACH #US NOT FAIR.

What's more, the white teachers don't teach the black students enough, like teaching them English, etc. They're motivated to teach white students, teaching and explaining but they overlook the fact that the black students are trying hard with English—They call on the teacher and are persistent; the teacher says wait a minute and gives a quick explanation, keeps her distance and goes back to the white children. Why? Finally, Thomas Bird was one black student who passed; all the white students go to Gallaudet while we black fail—that shows how the white teachers don't teach us enough—it's not fair.

SEGMENT #13

+M ⎯⎯⎯⎯⎯⎯⎯⎯⎯⎯⎯⎯⎯⎯⎯⎯⎯⎯⎯⎯⎯⎯→
  gaze down ·➤

MOST #OF #THEM MEAN REALLY NOT VERY MOTIVATED, REALLY

                              +M ⎯ "I am" ⎯⎯⎯⎯⎯⎯→
       gaze down   *cond*   *gaze down*

VERY MOTIVATED #IF MOTIVATED PRO:1 SURE GUARANTEE PRO:3

       gaze down   *neg*

LEARN,   BUT   MOTIVATED

Most of them are really not very motivated. If they were motivated, I'm sure they would learn, guaranteed. But they're not motivated.

SEGMENT #9

+M with voice ————————————————————"there is" ————————————————————————

#OK PRO:1 FEEL THAT THERE NOT ENOUGH QUALIFY CANDIDATES

"among the" ————————————————————— "mean they have a" ————————————————
                                                    gaze lf

AROUND   DEAF   COMMUNITY   LIMIT   BECAUSE   PRO:1

"have" ——————————————— "non" ————————————————————————————————

[F]IELD WORK N PROFIT [O]RGANIZATION MANAGE MENT HARD

"to" ——————————————— "who" ———————— "in that" ———————— "there" ————————

FIND   PEOPLE   EXPERIENCE   AREA   ARE EXAMPLE   WHILE

RUN   UNIVERSITY   REQUIRE   GREAT   EXPERIENCE   BACKGROUND

———————————————————————————— "am" ————————— "ing" ——— "they are" ———
          gaze down   *gaze down*

PRO:1   DON'T   FEEL   THAT   PRO:1   NOT   SAY   NOT

———————————————————————————————————— "they" ——————————— "I" ————————

ANY   QUALIFY   APPLICANTS   BUT   ARE   BUT   FEEL   THAT

"they are" ——————————————▶   +M ——————————▶
                                                    gaze rt

#SCARCE   NARROW   #NARROW   "YOUR TURN"-right

OK, I feel that there are not enough qualified candidates around the deaf community, I mean they have a limit because I have field-work experience in nonprofit organization management and it's hard to find people who have experience in that area . . . there are examples . . . while running a university requires great experience, background. I don't feel that . . . I am not saying that there aren't any qualified applicants but I feel that they are scarce . . . a limited selection. Now it's your turn.

Bibliography

Abdulaziz-Mkilifi, M. H. (1978). Triglossia and Swahili–English bilingualism in Tanzania. In J. Fishman (Ed.), *Advances in the study of social multilingualism* (pp. 129–152). The Hague: Mouton.

American Annals of the Deaf. (1852). Miscellaneous: Census of the deaf and dumb, **4**(4), 261–262.

Anisfield, M., and Lambert, W. (1963). Evaluation reactions of bilingual and monolingual children to spoken languages. *Journal of Social Psychology*, **69**, 82–97.

Aramburo, A. (1989). Sociolinguistic aspects of the black deaf community. In C. Lucas (Ed.), *The Sociolinguistics of the Deaf Community* (pp. 103–119). San Diego: Academic Press.

Baker, L. (1990). *The violation of phonological principles of ASL by invented signs in manual codes of English.* Unpublished manuscript, Gallaudet University, Department of Linguistics and Interpreting.

Battison, R. (1978). *Lexical borrowing in American Sign Language.* Silver Spring, MD: Linstok Press.

Beniak, E., Mougeon, R., and Valois, D. (1984/5). Sociolinguistic evidence of a possible case of syntactic convergence in Ontarian French. *Journal of the Atlantic Provinces Linguistics Association*, **6/7**, 73–88.

Bergman, E. (1976). Deaf students speak up: How they feel about the teaching and teachers of English. *Teaching English to the Deaf*, **3**(1), 4–14.

Berke, L. (1978). Attitudes of deaf high school students toward American Sign Language. In F. Caccamise and D. Hicks (Eds.), *Proceedings of the Second National Symposium on Sign Language Research and Teaching* (pp. 173–182). Silver Spring, MD: National Association of the Deaf.

Bernstein, M., Maxwell, M., and Matthews, K. (1985). Bimodal or bilingual communication? *Sign Language Studies*, **47**, 127–140.

Bokamba, E. G. (1985). *Code-mixing, language variation and linguistic theory: Evidence from Bantu languages.* Paper presented at the 16th Conference on African Linguistics. Yale University, New Haven, CT.

Bouchard-Ryan, E. (1973). Subjective reactions towards accented speech. In R. Shuy and R. Fasold (Eds.), *Language attitudes: Current trends and prospects* (pp. 60–73). Washington, D.C.: Georgetown University Press.

Brennan, E. M., Brennan, E. B., and Dawson, W. E. (1975). Scaling of apparent accentedness by magnitude estimation and sensory modality matching. *Journal of Psycholinguistic Research* **4**, 27–36.

Brill, R. G. (1974). *Education of the deaf, administrative and professional developments.* Washington, D.C.: Gallaudet College Press.

Brown, H. (1987). *Principles of language learning and teaching.* Englewood Cliffs, N.J.: Prentice-Hall.

Caccamise, F., and Hicks, D. (Eds.) (1978). American Sign Language in a bilingual, bicultural context. *Proceedings of the Second National Symposium on Sign Language Research and Teaching.* Silver Spring, MD: National Association of the Deaf.

Caccamise, F. (1980). *Introduction to interpreting.* Silver Spring, MD: RID Publications.

Caccamise, F., Garretson, M., and Bellugi, U. (Eds.). (1982). Teaching American Sign Language as a second/foreign language. *Proceedings of the Third National Symposium on Sign Language Research and Teaching.* Silver Spring, MD: National Association of the Deaf.

Chana, U., and Romaine, S. (1984). Evaluative reactions to Panjabi/English code-switching. *Journal of Multilingual and Multicultural Development,* **5**(6), 447–473.

Chiasson-Lavoie, M., and Laberge, S. (1971). *Attitudes face au français parlé à Montréal et degré de conscience de variable linguistique.* Unpublished research paper, McGill University.

Clerc, L. (1818). Address read at a public examination of the pupils in the Connecticut Asylum. Hartford, CT: Hudson.

Clyne, M. (1967). *Transference and triggering.* The Hague: Martinus Nijhoff.

Clyne, M. (1972). *Perspectives in language contact.* Melbourne: Hawthorne Press.

Clyne, M. (1982). *Multilingual Australia.* Melbourne: River Seine Publications.

Clyne, M. (1987). Constraints on code-switching. How universal are they? *Linguistics* **25**, 739–764.

Cokely, D. (1983). When is a pidgin not a pidgin? An alternative analysis of the ASL–English contact situation. *Sign Language Studies,* **38**, 1–24.

Corder, S. P. (1971). Idiosyncratic dialects and error analysis. *International Review of Applied Linguistics,* **9**, 147–159.

Corina, D., and Vaid, J. (1986). *Tapping into bilingualism: Cerebral lateralism for English and American Sign Language.* Paper presented at the Conference on Theoretical Issues in Sign Language Research, Rochester, NY.

Davies, S. (1991). *The Transition Toward Bilingual Education of Deaf Children in Sweden and Denmark: Perspectives on Language.* Gallaudet Research Institute Occasional Paper 91-1. Washington, D.C.: Gallaudet University.

Davis, J. (1989). Distinguishing language contact phenomena in ASL interpretation. In C. Lucas (Ed.), *The sociolinguistics of the deaf community* (pp. 85–102). San Diego: Academic Press.

Davis, J. (1990). *Interpreting in a language contact situation: The case of English-to-ASL interpretation.* Unpublished doctoral dissertation, University of New Mexico.

Davis, L., and Supalla, S. (1991). *A sociolinguistic description of signed language use among the Navajo.* Paper presented at the Colloquium on the Sociolinguistics of the Deaf Community, NWAVE XX, Georgetown University, Washington, D.C.

DeSantis, S. (1977). *Elbow to hand shift in French and American sign languages.* Paper presented at the annual NWAVE Conference, Georgetown University, Washington, D.C.

Deuchar, M. (1985). *British sign language.* London: Rutledge and Kegan Paul.

Dorian, N. (1981). *Language death. The life cycle of a scottish Gaelic dialect.* Philadelphia: University of Pennsylvania Press.

Edwards, V. (1986). *Language in a black community.* San Diego: College Hill Press.

Epée, C. M. (1776). *Institution des sourd muets par la voie des signes méthodiques.* Paris: Nyon. [Revised as Epée (1784). English translation (excerpts): *American Annals of the Deaf,* 1861, **13**, 8–29.]

Fasold, R. (1984). *The sociolinguistics of society.* Oxford: Basil Blackwell.

Ferguson, C. (1959). Diglossia. *Word,* **15**, 325–340.

Ferguson, C. (1966). National sociolinguistic profile formulas. In W. Bright, (Ed.), *Sociolinguistics* (pp. 309–315). The Hague: Mouton.

Ferguson, C. (1971). Absence of copula and the notion of simplicity. In D. Hymes (Ed.), *Pidginization and creolization of languages* (pp. 141–150). London: Cambridge Univ. Press.

Ferguson, C. (1975). Towards a characterization of English foreigner talk. *Anthropological Linguistics,* **17**, 1–14.

Ferguson, C., and DeBose, C. (1977). Simplified registers, broken language and pidginization. In A. Valdman (Ed.), *Pidgin and creole linguistics* (pp. 99–125). Bloomington: Indiana University Press.

Fischer, S. (1975). Influences on word-order change in American Sign Language. In C. N. Li (Ed.), *Word order and word order change* (pp. 1–25). Austin: University of Texas Press.

Fischer, S. (1978). Sign language and creoles. In P. Siple (Ed.), *Understanding language through sign language research* (pp. 309–331). New York: Academic Press.

Fishman, J. (1967). Bilingualism with and without diglossia; diglossia with and without bilingualism. *Journal of Social Issues,* **23**, 29–38.

Fishman, J. (1972). Varieties of ethnicity and varieties of language consciousness. In A. D. Dil (Ed.), *Language in sociocultural change* (pp. 179–191). Stanford, CA: Stanford University Press.

Friedman, L. (1976). The manifestation of subject, object and topic in American Sign Language. In C. N. Li (Ed.), *Word order and word order change* (pp. 125–148). Austin: University of Texas Press.

Frishberg, N. (1986). *Interpreting: An introduction*. Silver Spring, MD: RID Publications.

Gaies, S. (1977). The nature of linguistic input in formal second language learning: Linguistic and communicative strategies in ESL teachers' classroom language. In H. D. Brown, C. A. Yoris, and R. H. Crymes (Eds.), *Teaching and learning English as a second language: Trends in research and practice* (pp. 204–212). Washington, D.C.: Teaching English to Speakers of Other Languages.

Gal, S. (1979). *Language shift. Social determinants of linguistic change in bilingual Austria*. New York: Academic Press.

Gannon, J. (1981). *Deaf heritage. A narrative history of deaf America*. Silver Spring, MD: National Association of the Deaf.

Gerankina, A. (1972). *Practical work in sign language*. Moscow: Institute of Defectology.

Giles, H. (1977). *Language, ethnicity and intergroup relations*. London: Academic Press.

Graff, D., Labov, W., and Harris, W. A. (1986). Testing listeners' reactions to phonological markers of ethnic identity: A new method for sociolinguistic research. In D. Sankoff (Ed.), *Diversity and diachrony* (pp. 45–58). Amsterdam and Philadelphia: John Benjamines.

Grebler, L., More, J. W., and Guzman, R. C. (Eds.). (1970). *The Mexican American people*. New York: Free Press.

Groce, N. E. (1985). *Everyone here spoke sign language. Hereditary deafness on Martha's Vineyard*. Cambridge, MA: Harvard University Press.

Grosjean, F. (1982). *Life with two languages: An introduction to bilingualism*. Cambridge, MA: Harvard University Press.

Grosjean, F. (1989). Neurolinguistics, beware! The bilingual is not two monolinguals in one person. *Brain and Language, 36*, 3–15.

Grosjean, F. (1992). Another view of bilingualism. In Harris, R. J. (Ed.), *Cognitive processing in bilinguals*. Amsterdam: Elsevier.

Gumperz, J. J. (1962). Types of linguistic communities. *Anthropological Linguistics, 4*(1), 28–40.

Gumperz, J. J. (1964). Linguistic and social interaction in two communities. *American Anthropologist, 66*(6), (Part 2) 137–153.

Gumperz, J. J. (1982). *Discourse strategies*. London and New York: Cambridge University Press.

Gumperz, J. J., and Wilson, R. D. (1971). Convergence and creolization: A case from the Indo–Aryan–Dravidian border. In D. Hymes (Ed.), *The pidginization and creolization of languages* (pp. 151–169). Cambridge: Cambridge University Press.

Hatfield, N. (1982). *An investigation of bilingualism in two signed languages:*

American Sign Language and manually coded English. Unpublished Ph.D. dissertation, University of Rochester, NY.

Hatfield, N., Caccamise, F., and Siple, P. (1978). Deaf students' language competencies: A bilingual perspective. *American Annals of the Deaf*, **123**, 847–851.

Haugen, E. (1950). The analysis of linguistic borrowings. *Language* **26**, 210–231.

Haugen, E. (1953). *The Norwegian language in America: A study in bilingual behavior*. Philadelphia: University of Pennsylvania Press.

Haugen, E. (1956). *Bilingualism in the Americas: A bibliography and research guide*. Publications of the American Dialect Society, **26**.

Hayes, J. L. (1990). *A historical perspective and descriptive approach for American Sign Language and English bilingual studies in the community college setting*. Unpublished Ph.D. Dissertation, University of Arizona.

Herbert, R. (1982). Cerebral asymmetry in bilinguals and the deaf: Perspectives on a common pattern. *Journal of Multilingual and Multicultural Development* **3**, 47–59.

Hoover, M. R. (1978). Community attitudes toward Black English. *Language in Society* **7**, 65–87.

Jacobs, S. (1992). Coda Talk Column. *Coda Connection*, Vol. 9, no. 1.

Johnson, R. E. (1992). Sign language and the concept of deafness in a traditional Yucatec Maya village. In C. Erting (Ed.), *Proceedings of The Deaf Way*. Washington, D.C.: Gallaudet University Press.

Johnson, R. E. (1991). Sign Language, culture, and community in a Yucatec Mayan village. *Sign Language Studies* **73**, 461–478.

Johnson, R. E., Liddell, S., and Erting, C. (1989). *Unlocking the curriculum: Principles for achieving access in deaf education*. Gallaudet Research Institute Working Paper 89-3, Washington, D.C.: Gallaudet University Press.

Kachru, B. (1978). Toward structuring code-mixing: An Indian perspective. In B. Kachru and S. Sridhar (Ed.), *Aspects of sociolinguistics in South Asia*. Special issue, *International Journal of the Sociology of Language*, Vol. 16.

Kannapell, B. (1974). Bilingualism: A new direction in the education of the deaf. *Deaf American* **26**(10) 9–15.

Kannapell, B. (1985). *Language choice reflects identity choice: A sociolinguistic study of deaf college students*. Unpublished doctoral dissertation, Georgetown University, Washington, D.C.

Kannapell, B. (1989). An examination of deaf college students' attitudes toward ASL and English. In C. Lucas (Ed.), *The sociolinguistics of the deaf community* (pp. 191–210). San Diego: Academic Press.

Kelly, A. B. (1990). *Fingerspelling use among the deaf senior citizens of Baltimore*. Paper presented at NWAVE XIX, University of Pennsylvania, Philadelphia.

Kettrick, C. (1986). *Cerebral lateralization for American Sign Language and English on deaf and hearing native and nonnative signers*. Paper presented at Conference on Theoretical Issues in Sign Language Research, Rochester, NY.

Lambert, W. E., Hodgson, R. C., Gardner, R. C., and Fillenbaum, S. (1960).

Evaluation reactions to spoken languages. *Journal of Abnormal and Social Psychology* **60**, 44–51.

Lane, H. (1984). *When the mind hears*. New York: Random House.

Lee, D. M. (1982). Are there really signs of diglossia? Reexamining the situation. *Sign Language Studies* **35**, 127–152.

Lentz, E., Mikos, K., and Smith, C. (1988). *Signing naturally. Teacher's curriculum guide*. Berkeley, CA: Dawn Sign Press.

Liddell, S. (1980). *American Sign Language syntax*. The Hague: Mouton.

Liddell, S. K., and Johnson, R. E. (1989). American Sign Language: The phonological base. *Sign Language Studies* **64**, 195–278.

Lieberson, S. (1969). How can we describe and measure the incidence and distribution of bilingualism? In L. G. Kelly (Ed.), *Description and measurement of bilingualism* (pp. 286–295). Toronto: University of Toronto Press.

Light, R. Y., Richard, D. P., and Bell, P. (1978). Development of children's attitudes towards speakers of standard and nonstandard English. *Child Study Journal* **8**(4), 253–265.

Lincoln, P. C. (1979). Dual-lingualism: Passive bilingualism in action. *Te Reo* **22**, 65–72.

Lou, M. W. P. (1988). The history of language use in the education of the Deaf in the United States. In M. Strong (Ed.), *Language learning and deafness* (pp. 75–98). Cambridge: Cambridge University Press.

Lucas, C., and Valli, C. (1989). Language contact in the American deaf community. In C. Lucas (Ed.), *The sociolinguistics of the deaf community* (pp. 11–40). San Diego: Academic Press.

Lucas, C., and Valli, C. (1991). ASL or contact signing: Issues of judgment. *Language in Society* **20**, 201–216.

Mackey, W. F. (1967). *Bilingualism as a world problem/Le bilinguisme: phénomène mondial*. Montreal: Harvest House.

Mackey, W. F. (1968). The description of bilingualism. In J. Fishman (Ed.), *Readings in the sociology of language* (pp. 554–584). The Hague: Mouton.

Mather, S. (1991). The discourse marker OH in typed telephone conversations among deaf typists. Unpublished Ph.D. Dissertation, Georgetown University.

Meadow, K. P. (1972). Sociolinguistics, sign language and the deaf sub-culture. In T. J. O'Rourke (Ed.), *Psycholinguistic and total communication: The state of the art* (pp. 19–33). Washington, D.C.: American Annals of the Deaf.

Meath-Lang, B. (1978). A comparative study of experienced and nonexperienced groups of deaf college students: Their attitude toward language learning. *Teaching English to the Deaf* **5**(2), pp. 9–13.

Milroy, L. (1980). *Language and Social Networks*. Oxford: Basil Blackwell.

Moody, B. (1989). *International communication among deaf people*. Unpublished manuscript.

Moores, D. F. (1987). *Educating the deaf*. Boston: Houghton Mifflin.

Mougeon, R., and Beniak, E. (1987). The extra-linguistic correlates of core lexical borrowing. In K. M. Denning *et al.* (Eds.), *Variation in language: NWAV-XV at Stanford* (pp. 337–347). Stanford, CA: Stanford University Press.

Muench, E. (1971). Preliminary report: *Scaling of accentedness by magnitude estimation.* Unpublished manuscript, University of Notre Dame.

Mühlhäusler, P. (1986). *Pidgin and creole linguistics.* Oxford: Blackwell.

Myles-Zitzer, C. A. (1990). *A native deaf signer's foreign talk to hearing non-natives of American Sign Language.* Unpublished doctoral dissertation, University of California, Santa Barbara.

Neumann, Solow, S. (1981). *Sign language interpreting: A basic resource book.* Silver Spring, MD: NAD Publications.

Northrup, B. E., and Taff-Watson, M. (Eds.). (1987). *Workshop curriculum guides for interpreter trainers,* Vol. 1. RSA Region VI Interpreter Training Project. Little Rock: University of Arkansas.

Padden, C., and Markowicz, H. (1976). Cultural conflicts between hearing and deaf communities. In F. B. Crammatte and A. B. Crammatte (Eds.), *Proceedings of the Seventh World Congress of the World Federation of the Deaf* (pp. 407–411). Silver Spring, MD: National Association of the Deaf.

Palmer, L. A. (1973). A preliminary report on the study of the linguistic correlates of raters' subjective judgments on nonnative English speech. In R. Shuy and R. Fasold (Eds.), *Language attitudes: Current trends and prospects* (pp. 49–59). Washington, D.C.: Georgetown University Press.

Pap, L. (1949). *Portuguese–American speech: An outline of speech conditions among Portuguese immigrants in New England and elsewhere in the United States.* New York: King's Crown Press.

Platt, J. (1977). A model for polyglossia and multilingualism (with special reference to Singapore and Malaysia). *Language in Society* **6**, 361–379.

Poplack, S. (1980). Sometimes I'll start a sentence in English y termino en espanol: Toward a typology of code-switching. *Linguistics* **18**, 581–616.

Poplack, S., and Sankoff, D. (1988). Code-switching. In U. Ammon, N. Dittmar, and K. Mattheier (Eds.), *Sociolinguistics: An international handbook of language and society.* Berlin: Walter de Gruyter.

Poplack, S., Sankoff, D., and Miller, C. (1988). The social correlates and linguistic consequences of lexical borrowing and assimilation. *Linguistics,* Vol. 26, no. 1, pp. 47–104.

Poplack, S., Wheeler, S., and Westwood, A. (1987). Distinguishing language contact phenomena: Evidence from Finnish–English bilingualism. In P. Lilius and M. Saari (Eds.), *The Nordic languages and modern linguistics* Vol. 6 (pp. 35–56). Helsinki: University of Helsinki Press.

Preston, D. (1989). *Perceptual dialectology.* Dordrecht: Foris.

Reilly, J., and McIntire, M. (1980). American Sign Language and Pidgin Sign English: What's the difference? *Sign Language Studies* **27**, 151–192.

Richards, J. C. (1974). *Error analysis: Perspectives on second language acquisition.* London: Longman Group Ltd.

Rickford, J., and McNair-Knox, F. (1991). *Addressee- and topic-influenced style shift: A study in quantitative sociolinguistics.* Paper presented at NWAVE XX, Georgetown University, Washington, D.C.

Ries, P. (1973). *Further studies in achievement testing, hearing impaired students, Spring 1971.* Annual Survey of Hearing Impaired Children and Youth. Ser. D, No. 13. Gallaudet College Office of Demographic Studies, Washington, D.C.

Romaine, S. (1988). *Pidgin and Creole Languages.* London: Longman.

Romaine, S. (1989). *Bilingualism.* Oxford: Basil Blackwell.

Rosenthal, M. (1977). *The magic boxes: Children and Black English.* Arlington, VA: Center for Applied Linguistics.

Roy, C. (1989). *A sociolinguistic analysis of the interpreter's role in the turn exchanges of an interpreted event.* Unpublished doctoral dissertation, Georgetown University, Washington, D.C.

Rubin, J. (1968). *National bilingualism in Paraguay.* The Hague: Mouton.

Salisbury, R. E. (1962). Notes on bilingualism and linguistic change in New Guinea. *Anthropological Linguistics* **4,** 1–13.

Sankoff, D., Poplock, S., and Vanniarajan, S. (1986). The case of the nonce loan in Tamil. (Tech. Rep. 1348) University of Montreal, Centre de recherches mathématiques.

Schermer, T. M. (1990). *In search of a language. Influences from spoken Dutch on sign language of the Netherlands.* Delft: Eburon.

Scollon, R., and Scollon, S. (1979). *Linguistic convergence: An ethnography of speaking at Fort Chipewyan, Alberta.* New York: Academic Press.

Scotton, C. (1986). Diglossia and code-switching. In J. Fishman, A. Tabouret-Keller, M. Clyne, Bh. Krishnamurti, and M. Abdulazis (Eds.), *The Fergusonian Impact, Vol. 2; Sociolinguistics and the sociology of language* (pp. 402–416). Berlin: De Gruyter.

Selinker, L. (1972). Interlanguage. *International Review of Applied Linguistics* **10**(3), 209–231.

Shuy, R. W., Baratz, J., and Wolfram, W. (1969). *Sociolinguistic factors in speech identification* (Project Report No. MH 15048-01). Washington, D.C.: National Institute of Mental Health.

Smith, W. C. (1989). *The morphological characteristics of verbs in Taiwan Sign Language.* Unpublished doctoral dissertation, Indiana University.

Sridhar, S., and Sridhar, K. (1980). The syntax and psycholinguistics of bilingual code mixing. *Canadian Journal of Psychology* **34**(4), 407–416.

Stenson, N. (1974). Induced errors. In J. H. Schumann and N. Stenson (Eds.), *New frontiers of second language learning.* Rowley, MA: Newbury House.

Strevens, P. (1982). The localized forms of English. In B. Kachru (Ed.), *The other tongue. English across cultures* (pp. 23–30). Oxford: Pergamon Press.

Stokoe, W. C. (1969). Sign language diglossia. *Studies in Linguistics* **21,** 27–41.

Stokoe, W. C., Casterline, D., and Croneberg, C. (1965). *A dictionary of American Sign Language on linguistic principles* (New Ed.). Silver Spring, MD: Linstok Press.

Taff-Watson, M., and Duncan, J. (Eds.). (1987). Introduction to interpreting in legal settings. In M. Taff-Watson and B. E. Northrup (Eds.), *Workshop curriculum guides for interpreter training project* (pp. 63–118). Little Rock: University of Arkansas.

Taff-Watson, M., and Northrup, B. E. (Eds.). (1987). *Workshop curriculum guides for interpreter trainers*, Vol. 1. RSA Region VI Interpreter Training Project. Little Rock: University of Arkansas.

Taff-Watson, M., and Northrup, B. E. (Eds.) (1988). *University interpreter training curriculum guides*, Vol. 2. RSA Region VI Interpreter Training Project. Little Rock: University of Arkansas.

Tannen, D. (1986). Introducing constructed dialogue in Greek and American conversational and literacy narratives. In F. Coulmas (Ed.), *Reported speech across languages* (pp. 311–332). The Hague: Mouton.

Thelander, S. (1976). Code-switching or code mixing. *Linguistics* **183**, 103–123.

Thomason, S. G. (1983). Genetic relationship and the case of Ma'a (Mbugu). *Studies in African Linguistics* **14**, 195–231.

Thomason, S. G. (1984). *Is Michif unique?* Unpublished manuscript.

Thomason, S. G. (1986). Contact-induced change: Possibilities and probabilities. In W. Enninger and T. Stolz (Eds.), *Akten des 2. Essener Kolleguiumms zu Kreolsprachen und Srachkontakten* (pp. 261–284). Bochum: Studienverlag Dr. N. Brockmeyer.

Thomason, S., and Kaufman, T. (1988). *Language Contact Creolization and Genetic Linguistics*. Berkeley: University of California Press.

Thompson, R. M. (1975). Mexican–American English: Social correlates of regional pronunciation. *American Speech* **50**, 18–24.

Valli, C. (1988). *Language choice: Convergence and divergence*. Unpublished manuscript, Gallaudet University, Washington, D.C.

Valli, C., Prezioso, C., Lucas, C., Liddell, S., and Johnson, R. (1989). Open Letter to the Campus Community. Gallaudet University, Washington, D.C.

Valli, C., Reed, R., Ingram, N., and Lucas, C. (1990). *Sociolinguistic issues in the black deaf community*. Paper presented at The National Conferences on Employment and Black Deaf Persons, Lehman College, The Bronx, NY.

Ward-Trotter, J. (1989). An examination of language attitudes of teachers of the deaf. In C. Lucas (Ed.), *The sociolinguistics of the deaf community* (pp. 211–228). San Diego: Academic Press.

Weinreich, U. (1968). *Languages in contact*. The Hague: Mouton. (First Edition 1953. New York: Linguistic Circle of New York, Publication No. 2)

Weld, L. (1844). *Twenty-eighth Annual Report of the American Asylum at Hartford for the Education of the Deaf and Dumb* (p. 38). Hartford, CT.

Whinnom, K. (1971). Linguistic hybridization and the 'special case' of pidgins and creoles. In D. Hymes (Ed.), *Pidginization and creolization of languages* (pp. 91–115). London and New York: Cambridge University Press.

Williams, F. (1970). Psychological correlates of speech characteristics: On sounding "disadvantaged." *Journal of Speech & Hearing Research* **13**, 472–488.

Williams, F., Whitehead, J. L., and Miller, L. M. (1971). Ethnic stereotyping and judgments of children's speech. *Speech Monographs* **38**, 166–170.

Williams, F., Whitehead, J. L., and Traupmann, J. (1971). Teachers' evaluations of children's speech. *Speech Teacher* **20**, 247–254.

Witter-Merithew, A. (1982). The function of assessing as part of the interpreting process. *RID Interpreting Journal* **1**(2), 8–15.

Woodward, J. C. (1972). Implications for sociolinguistic research among the deaf. *Sign Language Studies* **1**, 1–7.

Woodward, J. C. (1973a). *Implicational effects of the deaf diglossic continuum.* Unpublished doctoral dissertation, Georgetown University, Washington, D.C.

Woodward, J. C. (1973b). Some characteristics of Pidgin Sign English. *Sign Language Studies* **3**, 39–46.

Woodward, J. C., and DeSantis, S. (1977). Two to one it happens: Dynamic phonology in two sign languages. *Sign Language Studies* **17**, 329–346.

Woodward, J. C., and Markowicz, H. (1975). *Some handy new ideas on pidgins and creoles: Pidgin sign languages.* Paper presented at Conference on Pidgin and Creole Languages, Honolulu, Hawaii.

Index

157